Roses in December

Marilyn Willett Heavilin

D0956934

THOMAS NELSON PUBLISHERS
Nashville

Published in Nashville, Tennessee, by Thomas Nelson, Inc., Publishers, and distributed in Canada by Word Communications, Ltd., Richmond, British Columbia, and in the United Kingdom by Word (UK), Ltd., Milton Keynes, England.

Unless otherwise noted, Scripture quotations are from The Holy Bible, KING JAMES VERSION.

Scripture quotations noted NASB are from THE NEW AMERICAN STANDARD BIBLE, Copyright © 1960, 1962, 1963, 1968, 1971, 1972, 1973, 1975, 1977 by The Lockman Foundation and are used by permission.

Scripture quotations noted RSV are from the REVISED STANDARD VERSION of the Bible. Copyright © 1946, 1952, 1971, 1973 by the Division of Christian Education of the National Council of the Churches of Christ in the U.S.A. Used by permission.

Scripture quotations noted NIV are taken from the HOLY BIBLE, NEW INTERNATIONAL VERSION ®. Copyright © 1973, 1978, 1984 by International Bible Society. Used by permission of Zondervan Bible Publishing House. All rights reserved.

The "NIV" and "New International Version" trademarks are registered in the United States Patent and Trademark Office by International Bible Society. Use of either trademark requires the permission of International Bible Society.

Scripture quotations noted TLB are from *The Living Bible* (Wheaton, Illinois: Tyndale House Publishers, 1971) and are used by permission.

Scripture quotations noted NKJV are from THE NEW KING JAMES VERSION. Copyright © 1979, 1980, 1982, Thomas Nelson, Inc., Publishers.

Library of Congress Cataloging-in-Publication Data

Heavilin, Marilyn Willett.
  Roses in December / Marilyn Willett Heavilin. — Rev. and expanded.
    p. cm.
  Includes bibliographical references.
  ISBN 0-8407-4440-4 (pbk.)
  1. Consolation. 2. Suffering—Religious aspects—Christianity. 3. Heavilin, Marilyn Willet. 4. Christian biography—United States. I. Title.
  [BV4905.2.H42 1993]
  248.8'6—dc20   92-39363
                                                   CIP

Printed in the United States of America
1 2 3 4 5 6 7 - 99 98 97 96 95 94 93

In Memory of
Jimmy, Nathan, and Ethan
Three beautiful flowers
in my bouquet of
December Roses

To Glen,
Matt and Debbie,
Mellyn and Mike
Your love and encouragement
have kept me going.

October 2, 1982 — Getting ready
for a cross-country race

February 15, 1983

Contents

From the Author

Dear Reader,

When I first wrote *Roses in December* in 1985-86, it was impossible for me to imagine how others would respond to the book. I simply knew I had to write—for me, for my family, to keep the memory of my sons alive, and more practically, to help me work through my own grief.

I was still too new in my grief to realize how universal my reactions to grief were. Now, eight years later, while I am pleased, I have learned not to be surprised when people tell me they could identify so completely with me as I described my own process.

Our sons Jimmy and Ethan died in infancy. When our son Nathan was killed by a drunk driver, I shouted to God through my pain, "Don't let this be wasted. It has to count. It must matter that Nathan, Jimmy, and Ethan Heavilin lived and that they died. Please don't let their lives be wasted."

This past year my husband and I had the privilege of being workshop leaders at the national convention of the Compassionate Friends, a support group for bereaved parents. It had been five years since we had spoken at a convention, so this was the first time we were able to receive many comments regarding *Roses in December*.

The first evening a woman walked up to me and said,

"I can't believe I'm getting to meet you. I'm alive because of you!" Naturally that statement caught my attention. As she started to tell me her story, I was overwhelmed. I asked her to write it out for me so that I could share her story with others and she happily obliged.

> I lost my only child, Lisa, on December 8, 1987. She died on her way to school, a passenger in a car driven by her "best friend." We received no support from her friend or her parents because we were told they were afraid we would sue. We lived in Pennsylvania because my husband was stationed there by the Marines. Our home was in Charleston, West Virginia. We took Lisa home [to West Virginia] for the last time. When we got back to Pennsylvania, no family, no Lisa, and we found no friends. As each day went on I wanted less and less to live. All our plans and dreams—as well as my future, my grandchildren—died with Lisa. I tried to talk my husband into a double suicide or a murder and suicide. How could we go on or want to?
>
> On a trip to West Virginia my dad took me to a Christian bookstore and bought me your book, *Roses in December*. I'm sure he wanted it because Lisa loved roses and she died in December. I took the book and read it in one sitting; then the next day I read it again. Finally I found a friend who understood and shared my feelings! I felt you knew my heartache of losing my only child because of your one-on-one relationship to your Nathan who died on February 10—my Lisa's birthday! My Lisa died in December; your Nathan was born in December.

How it must have hurt for you when you had to go to work at the school without Nathan there. I couldn't even drive by Lisa's school. How wonderful that you wrote a book for me out of your grief for Nathan. I felt for the first time my feelings were normal. I would grieve forever and it was okay.

On the anniversary of her death we sent roses to my parents and my five brothers and sisters with the message, "God gives us memories so we might have roses in December." They each took a rose that cold, sad day and put it on her grave since we were in Pennsylvania and couldn't be there for her. She will not be forgotten.

Thank you for your love. You saved my life with your compassion and caring!

Evelyn Ralston

During that convention I heard numerous comments similar to Evelyn's. Many said, "You gave me hope when I didn't want to live." Others stated, "We had hope for our marriage after we read *Roses in December*."

As I listened to each story, I heard God whisper in my ear, "It wasn't wasted. It matters that they lived and that they died."

Over 50,000 copies of *Roses in December* have been sold since its release in 1987. When my publisher asked that I update it, I read through it and realized there were very few changes to be made. My story hasn't changed, and my observations and opinions regarding the grief process have been confirmed over and over. I have included some recent comments from those who have read the book or heard me speak and updated personal information when it was pertinent. I have also included two additional chapters on subjects that I am asked to speak about frequently: the sovereignty of God and some additional information for caregivers.

The facilitator at the Compassionate Friends chapter we attend often opens the meeting by saying, "I am sorry each of you has a reason for coming here, but I am glad you have a place to come." May I paraphrase that statement to say, I am so sorry you have a need to read *Roses in December*, but since you do, I am grateful that such a book is available. I am comforted in knowing my grief has not been wasted.

Your friend and fellow sufferer,
MARILYN WILLETT HEAVILIN, 1993

The Rose
of
Preparation

Even when walking through the dark valley of death I will
not be afraid, for you are close beside me, guarding, guiding
all the way (Psalms 23:4 TLB).

I sat across the table from my friend Mary, silently sipping tea, waiting for her to speak. Her son had died just two weeks before. She started to speak several times, but her words were choked back by her sobs. Finally she took a deep breath and blurted out, "No one understands my grief. I feel so alone."

If you have recently experienced a heartbreak, perhaps you are also acquainted with the feelings of isolation and loneliness. It is true that no one else can understand your grief completely or feel your individual pain, but I have experienced loss. I've lived through my own grief: the disappointments, the shattered dreams, the fears, the depression, and the emotional pain that made my whole body ache. I remember feeling, too, that no one else could possibly understand, but I've discovered it is possible to walk through that long, cold winter season of grief and emerge on the other side a whole, healthy person.

Dear friend, you don't have to go through your grief alone. Please let me join you in this winter season and share my very special December roses with you.

The first rose along our path is the rose of preparation.

It was a cold, blustery February evening in 1943 when my mom and I climbed aboard the Greyhound bus and I excitedly waved goodbye to my daddy. We were going to a small town in northern Michigan to visit my grand-parents, my aunt and uncle, and best of all, my four-month-old cousin, Mary Beth. Now she would be old enough to respond to me. I could hardly wait. I'd been praying for a baby brother or sister as long as I could remember, but since my prayer hadn't been answered, I doted on cousin Mary Beth. As soon as Grandpa lifted me from the bus steps, I asked, "When can we see Mary Beth?" and was very disappointed when he said I'd have to wait until morning. I climbed in bed with Grandpa and Grandma before dawn and asked, "Can we go now?"

As I gobbled down my breakfast, I saw my aunt and uncle's truck coming up the lane. I anxiously met them at the door, but this unsuspecting, innocent five-year-old knew something was wrong when I saw the pain on their faces. Mary Beth wasn't with them. We all stood in that old farm kitchen with the snow piled high against the stone walls and windows, and my Uncle Louie began to explain. He told us that Mary Beth had suffocated in the night. She was dead.

I can still hear my own screams as I ran across the lane to my great-grandmother's home. "My baby's dead! My baby's dead!" My screaming must have torn at the breaking hearts of the adults, but no one reproved me. They just picked me up and hugged me as we cried together.

The snowstorm had closed the roads from town to my aunt's house, and when Uncle Louie had called the coroner and undertaker, he found out that they would have to wait for the snowplow—it could be hours before they arrived. Our family all drove to my aunt and uncle's cottage where a kind neighbor waited with Mary Beth's still form. I insisted on seeing "my baby," and no one had the strength to resist me. She had been a beautiful child, but the black and blue blotches that come with suffocation had stolen her beauty. I didn't care—she was still my Mary Beth.

I sat by the bed, stroked her hand, and talked to her. She felt like a china doll, cold and unresponsive. In those wintry hours my family was able to deal with their grief and to say goodbye privately to our sweet little Mary Beth. My fear of death waned as my mom explained that Jesus was taking care of Mary Beth and someday I would see her again. My fear of dead bodies lessened as I touched Mary Beth and realized she wasn't in that body anymore.

That was my first but not last contact with death as a child. By the time I was twelve, my paternal grandparents, my great-grandmother, a thirteen-year-old cousin, and a seventeen-year-old cousin had died. Even my Aunt Lucille and Uncle Louie died after their gas stove exploded, causing a flash fire. It was through that tragedy that I got my long-awaited little brother Walt—my parents adopted the youngest of Aunt Lucille and Uncle Louie's three orphaned children.

Death was no stranger to my family, but I don't look back to a childhood filled with tragedy and sad memories. I remember a family made strong through sorrow, a family with a tenacity that triumphed over troubles, and a family that cried and laughed together. After my husband Glen and I were married, we had three children, Matthew, Mellyn (our only girl), and Jimmy. Our life seemed ideal. Glen was an executive with General Motors, we had a new home, and we were on our way to a successful life.

Early one morning Glen went in to make a routine check on the children, but suddenly his voice penetrated my slumber, "Marilyn, call the doctor—Jimmy's gone."

With my heart pounding and my mind racing, I obediently called our personal friend and physician. "Tom, come quick, it's Jimmy!"

But I knew Glen must be mistaken. I quickly hung up the phone and raced into Jimmy's room in time to see Glen trying to breathe life into our young son. As my eyes fixed on Jimmy's lifeless form with black and blue blotches, I gasped, "Mary Beth!"

The memories came tumbling back in a wave. Could this be happening again? While waiting for the doctor, Glen and I knelt, with the baby still in his arms, and we prayed, "Jesus, please use this situation for Your honor and glory." The autopsy said "interstitial pneumonia." Today we would probably classify this as a crib death.

Jimmy died nearly thirty years ago, but as I write this account some scenes are still very vivid: the hurt I heard in my mother's voice as we called with the terrible news; the panic I felt later that day when the thought crossed my mind, *I haven't fed Jimmy!* And then the wave of grief as I realized Jimmy was dead; the feeling of rage mixed with overwhelming sadness that I experienced when I went into Jimmy's room and discovered that well-meaning friends had removed all of Jimmy's furniture and clothing without my knowledge or permission. I also recall dreading meeting people on the street or in the grocery store because I didn't want to answer the question, "How's your baby doing?"

Glen and I trusted the Lord and were able to go on with our lives, though it was hard when we were told, "You can still have lots of babies, and you'll probably forget all about this." A year and a half later we were delighted with the doctor's announcement that we were going to have twins. I reasoned that God was "paying us back" for the child He had taken. (It's amazing how we try to fit God into our mindsets.)

Our identical twin boys, Nathan James and Ethan Thomas, were born on Christmas morning, 1965. What a celebration we had! I received dozens of phone calls and bouquets. We were sure the birth of twins would lessen the pain of Jimmy's death.

We took Nathan home on New Year's Eve, but Ethan needed to gain a little weight. Each day I checked on Ethan and his progress was good. But on the ninth day his weight began going down and he was lethargic. Specialists were called in: diagnosis—pneumonia; prognosis—not good.

I was angry at life and at God. What had we done to deserve this? We were strong Christians, actively serving the Lord, and we had accepted Jimmy's death without bitterness or anger. Was this our thanks?

I struggled with God all night, and the next morning as I read out of *Streams in the Desert,* I thought I had found my answer. The verse for that day was "Go thy way; thy son liveth" (John 4:50).

I called all of my friends. "I'm sure Ethan will be fine. I'm sure that's what this verse means." Once again I thought I had God all figured out, but that evening as I pressed my face against the nursery window and watched my dear little Ethan labor with each breath, God spoke to me very clearly. "Marilyn, I loved you enough to die for you; aren't you willing to trust Me with this child?"

In an attempt to get alone with God, I went into the bathroom in the private room the hospital had given us, locked the door, slumped to the floor, and cried out to God. "This isn't fair. We're good people, good parents, good Christians. Why should this happen to us?"

Once I had blurted out my feelings, I sat silently for a while and then a peace began to grow within me. My prayer continued, "Lord, I don't understand this, and I certainly don't like it. But I love You and I trust You. I give You complete control over Ethan's life. Now You must give me the strength to live through this." A few minutes later Ethan joined his brother Jimmy in heaven.

I leaned my head heavily against Glen's shoulder as we drove home silently. The snow glistened in the moonlight and I could hear the crunch of our tires against the frozen slush on the highway. My mind drifted back to that verse, "Go thy way; thy son liveth." What did it mean to me now?

Glen and I were in the process of joining a Christian organization in California. We were leaving our home, our family, and our friends. I *sensed* God was saying through that verse, "Marilyn, continue with your plans; serve Me with all your heart; and don't worry about Ethan or Jimmy. They're both living with Me, and they're fine."

I now believe that was what God was saying, but I couldn't *receive* that interpretation until I had yielded *my* will to His. I experienced many of the same adjustments after Ethan died as I had after Jimmy's death. We had already sent out birth announcements and an article had appeared in our local paper so during the first few weeks after Ethan died, we often received congratulation cards and sympathy cards in the same mail. I recall receiving two beautiful baby blue suits accompanied with a note,

"Twins! I think you're one of the luckiest couples in the world!"

I didn't feel lucky; I felt plagued because our troubles were continuing. Shortly after Jimmy died I began to have a problem with recurring ovarian cysts, which required several surgeries. Five weeks after Ethan died the pain began again. I had another cyst. We consulted several doctors, who all recommended that I have a total hysterectomy. After losing two babies in less than two years, the hope for more children was gone. While some of my friends were crying because of too many pregnancies, I was crying because I would never be pregnant again.

A month after that surgery, my grandmother died. As the family was preparing to leave the house for Grandma's funeral, Glen developed a migraine headache and went to bed. Then I began sobbing so violently someone had to give me a tranquilizer to calm me down enough that I could attend the funeral.

People couldn't understand why Glen and I were having such a difficult time with my grandmother's death. After all, she was in her seventies, she had lived a good life, and she didn't suffer long. None of us took time to consider what Glen and I had been through in the past year and a half. And the following year we moved four times, including one move from Indiana to California.

We moved from a large home into a tiny, two bedroom apartment with rented furniture, and Matt and Mellyn were to sleep in bunkbeds with Nate's crib in the same tiny room. The very first evening Glen had to work late so I began trying to get Matt and Mellyn settled into bed by myself. Just as they climbed in, the top bunk came crashing down on top of Mellyn! Except for a few bumps and bruises, she was not injured, but the children all became hysterical. Overwhelmed and crying myself, I collapsed in the middle of the floor and tried to comfort my three screaming children, all the while thinking, *and this is the great adventure God has called me to?*

When Nate was about eight months old, I went into a severe depression. I couldn't sleep; I cried a lot; and when I wasn't crying I was yelling at the children. Glen was very patient with me but he didn't know what was wrong. My Christian friends were certain it was a spiritual problem, and they kept asking, "Are you sure you understand the Spirit-filled life?"

My mother came to visit, took one look at me, and said, "This girl needs to go to bed." I had been running and running from my pain, but it finally caught up with me. No one had warned me that it was necessary to grieve, nor did anyone explain that even though I had a baby and two other children to take care of, I would still miss Jimmy and Ethan. I was told that the adjustment to a hysterectomy was all in my head, and I was not informed about the changes that would occur in my body. Three babies, two funerals, four surgeries, and four moves in twenty-four months and I was only twenty-seven. No wonder I was depressed!

My mother gave me the physical help I needed, the children matured, and I slowly grew accustomed to my grief. As the years went by and I spent my time with my family, God allowed the empty spots in my heart to be filled to some extent by other children, especially boys, who needed the attention I had time to give.

We cooked for the band and bolstered the high school football team. Matt and Mellyn participated in various activities, and Glen, Nate, and I became their cheering section. Matt and Mellyn graduated and went on to college. In 1982, Mellyn married Mike Savage, a young man I had led to the Lord earlier.

That fall Nate began his junior year in high school. He had grown into a tall, handsome, sixteen-year-old young man. He was on the cross-country and basketball teams, sang in the ensemble, played trumpet in the pep band, and was on the honor roll. Since I worked at the Christian high school he attended, Nate and I spent a lot of time together driving to and from school. Although he was a very quiet boy, occasionally he shared something that gave me a hint of what was going on in his mind.

One morning as we were driving to school, he said, "Mom, have you ever wondered what Ethan looks like?"

I said, "Well, honey, you were identical twins; he must look just like you."

There was quiet for a moment, and then Nate said wistfully, "Boy, I sure would like to see him."

I chuckled rather uneasily trying to cover up the strange feeling that flooded over me and replied, "Well, when we get to heaven, we'll all get to see him and Jimmy, too."

The Rose of Sorrow

And now, dear brothers, I want you to know what happens to a Christian when he dies so that when it happens, you will not be full of sorrow, as those are who have no hope (1 Thessalonians 4:13 TLB).

On February 10, 1983, as we arrived at school, Nate scurried off with his friends to leave for a field trip. The day before I had heard him ask his brother Matt, "Hey, brother, how would you like to take a day off work?"

Nate explained that his class was going to Los Angeles and they needed more cars and drivers. I wasn't surprised when Matt agreed to drive. He was always a softy when it came to his little brother. Nate hardly had time to talk with me between his return from the field trip and leaving for the evening's basketball game. In fact, he was trotting backward down the hall when I asked him what time he would be home.

"Oh, I don't know. The game might run kinda late, and it will take a while for the drive home. I'll call you if we're going to be really late."

He gave a quick wave, and called, "See ya later, Mom," as he dashed to his locker to get his uniform and gym bag.

That night my husband, Glen, went to his college class, and I spent a quiet evening alone. My mom called from San Diego where she and Dad were camping with some friends, and Mellyn called to check on details of the homecoming game the next evening at Nate's school. As I tried to watch television, I kept falling asleep, so I finally went to bed and slept soundly. Suddenly, I awoke. Where was I? Why wasn't Glen in bed with me? My thoughts were all jumbled. What time was it? My sleep-blurred eyes eventually focused on the clock. 11:44.

I hurried down the hall to find Glen. "Isn't Nate home yet?" Glen shook his head. With much uneasiness, I said, "Something must be wrong. He always calls if he's going to be late." I tried to appear calm for Glen, but on the inside, I was crying, *Please bring him home, Lord; please bring him home.*

At first we hesitated to call anyone. Surely it is just car trouble; he'll call us soon, we reasoned. This was a new experience for us. Nate was always good about calling. My pride made it difficult for me to call others and admit I didn't know where my son was. But as it grew later and later, alarm overruled pride.

After several calls to Nate's coaches, we tried calling a friend who always rode with Nate. The sick feeling in my stomach grew when there was no answer at his house. I thought, *his family never stays out late; they must have heard something. Why haven't we?*

Glen called another of Nate's friends, but her mom answered. Soon I heard Glen say, "What hospital are they in?" As Glen was dialing the hospital, he said, "There's been a terrible head-on collision. All of the kids who were in Nate's car are in the hospital."

The emergency room attendant told Glen they had a young male, listed as John Doe. I heard Glen say, "Does that mean he's dead?"

"He's alive but he's unconscious and unable to identify himself." The attendant continued, "Mr. Heavilin, come quickly." I knocked on Matt's bedroom door, "Honey, there's been a bad accident. Get dressed quickly; we must hurry!"

Matt recalls: "Mom didn't say who was in the accident. Grandma and Grandpa Willett were out of town that night—it could have been them. But I knew it was Nate. As I was numbly getting dressed, I thought, 'We're going through another funeral.'" At twenty-four Matt was already well acquainted with grief.

It seemed I was moving in slow motion. I desperately needed to get to Nate and kept telling myself everything would be all right once we got there. I knew if I could touch him and speak to him, he would wake up.

In my mind, I was talking to Nate all the while I was dressing. *Hang on, Nate. I'm coming; I'm coming. Just hang on.* Our minds were in a fog, but we were functioning automatically in an organized manner. Matt remembered to take rolls of coins for phone calls, and I grabbed my address book thinking, *We've got to call everybody and tell them to pray.* Then I thought of Glen's and my parents. How could we tell them Nate might be dying? Grandchildren aren't supposed to die.

It was the middle of the night and everything seemed so still. We passed the parents of one of the girls who'd been in Nate's car, heading to another hospital. We rolled down the car windows to exchange information.

"How's your daughter?" we asked.

"She's conscious and has many facial injuries. How's Nate?"

"He's unconscious—listed as a John Doe. Pray!"

As Glen drove, I prayed. The first part of my prayer was simply, "God, is it happening again? We've already lost two children. Do we have to bear that pain again?"

At the hospital we hurried to the reception desk. "Where's Nate? How is he? Can we see him?" So many questions and no answers. The nurse just said, "Someone will be out to see you shortly; please fill out these forms."

We struggled to focus our minds on car license numbers and insurance information. Finally Glen talked with a police officer who verified the car involved in the crash was ours, but told us nothing about Nate. He said the accident occurred at 11:44, the exact time I had awakened so suddenly! How thankful I am God awakened me so we were able to get to the hospital before it was too late.

A security guard appeared, saying, "Clear the halls. We're bringing a patient through." We stood in a doorway to watch. Several people huddled over the person on the cart, but I could see a head of tousled brown hair, a pair of blue jeans, and a big foot wearing a white sock. Just as the cart was pushed out of sight, I realized it was Nate.

I wanted to run after him, but instead I just stood there, numb, trying to take in what I had seen. My son, my Nate, lying on that cart, so helpless; my son who had looked anything but helpless as he grabbed his uniform and left for a physically taxing evening of basketball.

"Oh God, please help him; please help us," I whispered.

Soon a nurse called us into a small, cluttered office, and in a warm, but very concerned voice, she said, "We have just taken your son to surgery. His leg has been crushed; he has brain damage and extensive damage to his heart and lungs. His heart stopped once already, and we opened his chest to massage the heart and start it again."

I felt sick as I envisioned someone's hands on my son's heart. My thoughts drifted back to the prayer I had prayed on the way to the hospital. "Lord, please don't let it be Nate's fault. Please heal all of the kids if it's Your will. Lord. . . ."

I hesitated and began again, "Lord, we want Your will in Nate's life, and Lord, we're giving You power of attorney over Nate."

As the nurse continued, I began to sense what God's will was for Nate. I asked the nurse, "Do you think he's going to make it?" Her eyes dropped, and she shook her head, "No." A kind-looking woman came up to me and said, "My brother was the driver of the other car. I'm so sorry. I'm so sorry. Is your son going to be all right?"

I answered very matter-of-factly, "My son is dying." As she began to weep, I instinctively wrapped my arms around her and said, "It's okay. If Nate dies, I know he'll go to heaven and I'll see him again someday."

The lady stiffened a little and walked away. Perhaps my comments seemed too unfeeling, too calloused. They weren't meant to be. I realize now I was in the numbness of grief. God was speaking for me. As Mellyn and Mike arrived, we hugged each other tightly, prayed, and waited.

Eventually we learned that the three other students in Nate's car were seriously injured, but the doctors said they would survive. A prayer answered. We also had learned the man who hit Nate had been arrested for drunk driving. I experienced anger and relief at the same time. It wasn't Nate's fault, another prayer answered, but my son was dying because someone had been foolish enough to drink and drive. My son, who never drank and who was from a family who didn't drink, was the victim of a drunk driver. How unfair!

The words "drunk driver" were still spinning in my mind as the nurse reentered the waiting room. When I saw her face, I knew. "Is he gone?" She nodded. Glen came from around the corner, and I said, "Honey, he's gone."

The hope left his eyes as he hugged me tightly and we wept. Ten years have passed since that agonizing evening, years filled with a mélange of emotions and questions. Why our son? Why did he have to die? Will the sick feeling in my stomach ever go away? Why didn't we at least have time to say goodbye?

I have felt anger at a justice system that doesn't protect us from such happenings; jealousy toward others whose lives seem to go untouched; resentment that it was my son instead of someone else's. However, as I walked into Nate's memorial service and saw nearly a thousand people in attendance, I realized that God had allowed Nate to touch more lives in seventeen years than many of us touch in seventy; many of them young lives, people who can still have years of service for God. Even now as I reread the numerous newspaper articles, including one with the headline: "Nathan lives now in his heavenly, not Heavilin, home," I feel confident that Nate was a witness to the entire community for his Lord Jesus, in his life and in his death.

His death also caused some adults to change their priorities. After Nate died, a coworker of Glen's began attending his own son's track meets regularly—time with his son has become very precious.

A few weeks later a college representative was in my office and I shared my story with her. She asked, "Considering what you've just been through, do you have any specific advice for other parents?"

I responded, "Spend all of the time you can with your family. Always keep them on the top of your priority list." The next day she wrote me a letter.

"I want you to know that as a result of my conversation with you on Wednesday, I've canceled all my appointments for today and I'm going home to my son—first to attend his baseball game, then home to be with him."

I quickly saw God allowing us to influence lives around us because of our experience. One month after Nathan's death, some of my students and I visited Biola University. As we rested in our dorm room we talked about what it was going to be like living without Nate. They commented:

"It's no fun at school anymore."

"I don't like to watch the basketball games now."

"How can we ever enjoy Christmas again since Nate's birthday is Christmas Day?"

I muttered, "I'd like to ask God to cancel December because I don't want any part of Christmas." The thought of gifts, Christmas carols, and Christmas programs seemed incongruous with what we were facing.

The next morning the students visited classes, and my friend Diana and I wandered around the campus, ending up at the bookstore. I was aimlessly leafing through the display of posters when one caught my eye. I couldn't believe it. Through my tears, I called to Diana, "Come and look at this!" The poster was of a beautiful red rose. The flower had opened and dewdrops were visible on the petals. At the bottom was a quote which conveyed a message from God to me that day. It read,

"GOD GIVES US MEMORIES SO WE MIGHT HAVE ROSES IN DECEMBER."[1]

My first thought was, *God, You've got to be kidding. Even in California we don't find many roses in December, and there certainly aren't any roses in my life right now.* But I bought the poster, had it framed, and hung it in my bedroom. I glanced at it frequently and seemed to hear God say,

"Marilyn, I'm not going to cancel December, but I've given you many, many wonderful memories of Nate. Gather and savor them because through those memories and through the special things I'm going to do for you this year and every year, you're going to have bouquets of roses, even in December.

"Keep looking for the roses!"

God is continually keeping His promise by providing roses, sometimes with actual flowers, sometimes through friends, and often in the form of memories as a reminder He is caring for me, and when I hurt, He hurts.

A few months later I was helping a student with a scholarship notebook she had compiled. It included certificates showing her accomplishments, and pictures from high school yearbooks. I turned to a page with a group picture, and I didn't see anything else, only that Nate was in the picture. When I saw it, I was overwhelmed with sorrow and began to cry.

At that moment, Sally, the school secretary, came into my office unaware of what had just happened. She was holding a rose. She explained, "I bought this rose for someone else, but she isn't here today, and God just told me I should bring it to you!" In the years since Nate's death, hardly a moment has gone by without my thinking of him. Knowing that God cares doesn't take the hurt away, but it does make the hurt bearable. We have gathered many memories, each a beautiful rose.

One of my young friends, Darcy, gave me a notepad which states, "A rose is God's autograph." As I stroll in my rose garden of memories, I see God's autograph everywhere. Each rose is a special, signed gift from God reminding me of His care. And when the hurts become more than I can bear, it seems He always sends me another rose—a beautiful memory or a precious friend. God continues to increase my bouquet of roses. Some have come with thorns, but God has helped me deal even with the thorns.

Perhaps you are going through a December in your life: a death, a divorce, or some other severe disappointment, and you can't see any roses. Let me share my December roses with you so you can start collecting a bouquet of your own and then share your roses with others.

The Rose of Comfort

Rejoice with them that do rejoice, and weep with them that weep (Romans 12:15).

When we left the hospital after Nathan's death, the many friends who were waiting for us wanted to know, "What can we do for you?" My response was, "Come home with us," because we did not want to walk into our house alone. We arrived at our home after 3:00 A.M., and within an hour more than forty people were with us sitting in our living room having a prayer meeting.

Their friendship, even in the middle of the night, comforted me immeasurably. As we prayed, I sensed we were not the only ones who were grieving—we were not the only ones who would miss Nathan.

I will always remember my friend Donna Lynn's prayer because she thanked God for the memories and asked Him to help us concentrate on the good times. Her prayer came from the heart of one mother and touched the heart of another. At that moment, all I could remember were the times I had been upset with Nate and had made wrong decisions, but Donna Lynn's prayer helped me focus on the good times. I began to see that even though there were a few times I would like to have changed, the good memories far outweighed the not-so-good ones. Her positive prayer was an encouragement and a comfort.

Early that morning, Vonette Bright arrived. After speaking at a prayer breakfast where she had shared about our tragedy, she came directly to our home.

Following her message, a young couple had come to her and said, "Vonette, we have a verse we would like you to take to your friend." When Vonette arrived at our home, she was excited even though she was broken for us. The verse reads: "The good men perish; the godly die before their time. . . . No one seems to realize that God is taking them away from evil days ahead. For the godly who die shall rest in peace" (Isa. 57:1-2 TLB).

Five people shared the same verse with us by noon that day. Later I discovered J. Vernon McGee had preached from that text that morning on the radio. Since his program is broadcast at 7:30 A.M. in this area, many of our friends were listening to Dr. McGee when they received the news about Nathan. What timing!

Through this verse, God said to me, "Marilyn, it wasn't an accident. I wasn't on vacation the night Nate died. I knew about it before it happened. Marilyn, I'm taking him away from something worse. He's with Me, and he's doing fine."

Over the years I've observed that, for the Christian, there are many things worse than death. I may not know until eternity all that God spared Nathan, but I can rest assured from now until then that Nate is with the Lord, and he is doing fine. I am so thankful Vonette took the time to visit me. My whole outlook might have been different if I hadn't received her comforting words.

However, not all the words we received were comforting. Have you ever, in your eagerness to be helpful, said something that you realized afterward could cause problems? One well-meaning lady heard my story and suggested we have someone pray over us to cleanse our bloodlines! Another listener suggested our family was bound by a curse of death. After the death of each of my children at least one person suggested we confess the sin in our lives or that we needed more faith. I have begun to understand that most of these comments are motivated out of fear that the same thing could happen to those who share them. If a person can come up with a reason for your trauma, they can believe if they avoid that particular pitfall, nothing similar will happen to them.

While we were waiting at the hospital, I received a phone call from an acquaintance asking how Nate was doing. By then God had confirmed in my heart that Nate wasn't going to live, so I simply said, "Nate is dying." I expected her response to be similar to ours, feeling hurt, crushed, and disappointed. It wasn't.

She exclaimed, "Oh no, you can't give up. Death comes from Satan. If you give up, you're giving in to Satan, and if Nate dies, it will be because you gave up."

As I hung up the phone, I saw the nurse coming to tell us Nate was dead. The words rang in my ears, "Nate died because you gave up."

As we walked out of the hospital into the parking lot, I asked God to give me a verse to comfort me. Part of one verse, "Precious in the sight of the Lord is the death of his saints" (Ps. 116:15 RSV), and the principle taught in another, that even before we are formed, our days are numbered (Ps. 139:16), came to me immediately.

Later, however, the woman's words came back to haunt me again and again. Glen helped me resolve the matter when he said, "Marilyn, you never gave up on Nate, you gave *over* to God."

Glen was right. He reminded me of the prayer I had prayed on the way to the hospital. "God, we give You power of attorney in Nathan's life. We trust he is going to be fine, but if that isn't Your will, it's okay. We are turning the controls over to You."

Whenever I saw this lady after Nate's death, I had to remind myself, "I didn't give up; I gave over." In my heart, I was sure I hadn't given up on Nate, but I knew she still thought I had. I wanted to cry every time I saw her. Her words put a wall between us which could not be torn down easily.

"It is harder to win back the friendship of an offended brother than to capture a fortified city. His anger shuts you out like iron bars" (Prov. 18:19 TLB).

For those who want to comfort others, I would caution that you be sensitive. When you are talking with those who are going through trauma, allow for the work that God is doing in their hearts, and take your cue from what they say.

In our case, God was very clearly preparing us for Nathan's death even as we drove to the hospital. He was working with us and planting peace in our hearts. Those who were close to us sensed it immediately. Nate didn't die because we had "given up"; Nate died because God said, "I miss you, Nate; come on home."

It is very important to acknowledge a person's loss quickly, through a note, a card, or a personal visit, but don't feel you must explain or justify the trauma. Of all the ways you can help those in crisis, offering "words of wisdom" can be the most risky. Even if your suggestions or philosophy are positive, they may not be accepted in a positive manner by those in the middle of a trauma.

Dr. Henry Brandt has been my personal friend for over forty years, and we have been through many trials together. I trust him and often ask for his counsel. Uncle Henry, as I fondly call him, spent the weekend with us after Nate's death. I was glad.

Each time I began to get upset because of the circumstances we were facing, Uncle Henry would lovingly put his arm around me, hug me, and say, "Let the peace of God rule in your heart" (Col. 3:15).

His words were scriptural—but each time he hugged me and made me the benefactor of his spiritual insight, I got angry. I knew what he was trying to say. He was pointing out that my peace should come from Christ and not from my circumstances, but I didn't want to hear it. My son was dead; why should I want peace?

Fortunately, Dr. Brandt and I knew each other well enough that he could risk my anger. As my anger dwindled, through Uncle Henry's words I was able once again to ask God for His peace so that I could face this December of my life victoriously.

My rule of thumb when talking to a bereaved person is: If you don't know what to say, if you aren't sure how God is working in the situation, just hug the person. Offer advice only sparingly. If you are the one who is suffering, and if people have said things that seem insensitive or do not help or comfort when you are grieving, ask God to guide your response. It is unlikely they meant to be unkind; in fact, as in Dr. Brandt's case, they may be saying what you need to hear. Try to learn from the experience and be sensitive and compassionate as you deal with others.

Before you try to console with words, make sure you have already established a good rapport with the bereaved, and don't be offended if your advice is not immediately accepted. I'm glad Dr. Brandt was willing to take the risk, and I'm also thankful he stuck with me even when I didn't want to accept his advice.

As comforters, we should tread softly. Sometimes there isn't anything we can say except, "I love you; I'm praying for you, and I'm here for you."

"From a wise mind comes careful and persuasive speech" (Prov. 16:23 TLB).

Let me suggest some other forms of encouragement and comfort you can offer which may minimize your risk of saying the wrong thing.

In spite of sorrow, people still need to eat, but few bereaved people have the motivation or strength to prepare meals for themselves. If you like to cook and have the time, your favorite dish will be much appreciated by a grieving family.

You don't have to be a gourmet cook to help. Shortly after breakfast on that fateful Friday morning, my friend Jackie arrived with a sack of groceries: cheese, crackers, bread, cinnamon rolls, other snacks, napkins, and paper plates. This helped tremendously.

Several years ago the teenage son of a man who served on a church board with Glen died very suddenly. I felt we should visit the family right away, but since we didn't know them well, I was a little nervous. I took a loaf of homemade bread out of my freezer, thinking, *Even if they don't want to see us, they'll like my bread.* We went to their door. A friend of the family welcomed us, accepted the bread, and invited us in.

We found the family and their close friends so dazed by the circumstances surrounding the boy's death that no one seemed able to think about what needed to be done. I asked, "Has the pastor been called?"

"No."

"Have friends been called?"

"No."

No plans had been made for meals or for accommodations for relatives who would be coming from out of town. When I asked if I could stay and help with some of those details, they readily accepted.

Glen returned home to take care of our children and I stayed until late that evening. I returned daily for the next several days to help with funeral arrangements, make phone calls, and plan meals, and the mother even asked me to help her clean out their son's room. A simple loaf of bread had opened the door and made it possible for me to see needs and help a family in a very vital way.

One act of kindness I particularly appreciated was when people brought pictures they had taken of Nathan. Some were of events we had also photographed but were different poses or groupings. Others laminated newspaper articles of the accident and funeral for us.

Several of Nathan's classmates cleaned our house the week after Nate's death. Two of them, Debbie and Julie, offered to come on a weekly basis for the remainder of the school year. What a blessing!

I am an organized person and under normal circumstances would have no trouble keeping my house clean, but during this time, cleaning a bathroom or running a vacuum was of little importance to me. I used all of the strength I had just to function at work. When I got home I collapsed into a chair. I didn't have the emotional or physical strength to do much cleaning or cooking. I am so grateful these girls saw my need and were willing to commit themselves to help.

God also had a special bonus in store for all of us through this. Two years later Debbie became my daughter-in-law! We both look back to her "house-cleaning days" as a wonderful time for a future mother-in-law and daughter-in-law to get to know each other. Debbie is one of our very beautiful and special roses.

We received more than six hundred cards and letters after Nathan's death, and they still comfort me. The cards with personal notes were especially meaningful.

Many people chose to telephone us rather than to come to the house. This was fine, but often I could not talk long because of all the activity in our home, and I was sorry I couldn't reach out and hug those people.

Some people sent telegrams of condolences and we appreciated their thoughtfulness. We also appreciated the flowers and plants that came to the house. They were lovely reminders of those who grieved with us.

There are a number of details connected with funeral arrangements which will need to be taken care of, and I have put together a checklist which I hope will be helpful. Many of these things can be done by a close friend or family member.

__Call the pastor
__Call relatives
__Call family attorney
__Locate any existing will
__Call insurance companies
__Locate all insurance policies and bank accounts
__Check on existing retirement funds
__Notify Social Security
__Help write obituary
__Help plan funeral
__Go with bereaved to mortuary and cemetery
__Provide guest book to use at bereaved's home
__Find someone to provide family meals
__Clean the house
__Mow the lawn
__Grocery shop (especially for munchies and finger foods, paper products: tissues, toilet tissue, towels, plates, cups, napkins, etc.)
__Do minor house and car repairs

__Have someone stay at house during funeral

__Have someone record food and flowers brought to
the home.

The evening after the accident was our school's first
homecoming event. Nate and the other boy injured in the
accident both played trumpet in the pep band. How can
a pep band be peppy without trumpets? Helen, a mother
of students at the school, and an accomplished trumpet
player, asked herself that question and came up with a
solution.

She stopped by our house and said, "If you'll give me
Nate's music, I would like to play the trumpet for him
tonight at Homecoming if it's okay with you." Helen
found a unique way to help in our time of need.

Shortly after Nathan's death I attended the funeral of
another young man killed by a drunk driver. Someone
had put together a photo album of pictures portraying
his life. In addition, a collage of pictures was displayed
on an easel—beautiful memories for us all to enjoy. What
a special tribute.

This man left a young son who had had very little time
to collect memories of his daddy. As we entered the
viewing room at the funeral home, a nicely printed note
was placed on a table along with blank pages of paper.
The note asked us to write about a memory we had of the
deceased. These were to be placed in a notebook to be
given to his son when he is old enough to appreciate it.
That notebook will give the son a much-needed link to
the father he never knew.

After my friend Barbara's house burned in a Southern
California fire, she recalled: "One friend went through
her entire house and boxed up a wide assortment of
things that she felt she would need if she had nothing.
She brought items from shampoo and bobby pins to

towels and face cloths and even flannel pajamas for my husband.

"At Christmas one young man brought an umbrella, jigsaw puzzles for our family, and tools for my husband.

"One dear lady who is extremely shy came by with some lovely clothes (some brand new) in the exact size I needed, and when she was gone we discovered rolls and a pie and all sorts of other special things. I'm not sure she ever said a word, but we will never forget what her actions said."

When another friend and her children were trying to recover from an unexpected and unwanted divorce, she greatly appreciated the families who invited her children on outings with them. She also recalls how often she wished for someone to do needed repairs around the house or simple maintenance work on the car.

I have one I-wish-we-would-have-done-that suggestion. It would have been helpful later if we had had a guest book at our home to record the names of friends who came or brought in food. Several hundred people came through our home that week, and I wish I had a way of remembering all of them.

I also wish someone could have helped us think in those hours just after Nate's death. Glen and I both regret that we weren't able to donate some of Nate's organs to a needy person, and we are sorry we didn't ask to see Nate at the hospital after he died. Now we realize that neither of us had been convinced absolutely that it was really Nate until we saw his body in the casket. We had both wanted to see him at the hospital, but weren't able to verbalize our thoughts.

When you are with the bereaved, be a good listener. Encourage them to express themselves freely. Don't reprove them for what they say or feel, but help them voice their feelings, and try to understand them. We often tend to stay away when friends hurt because we can think of no specific way to help. After Nathan's death, I discovered that the little things meant as much as the big things. Even when we are in the midst of grief ourselves, we can be a rose to others around us who are hurting if we are willing to be sensitive to their needs.

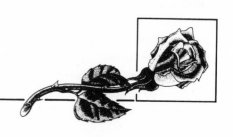

The Rose
of
Forgiveness

Let all bitterness, and wrath, and anger, and clamour, and evil speaking, be put away from you, with all malice: And be ye kind one to another, tenderhearted, forgiving one another, even as God for Christ's sake hath forgiven you (Ephesians 4:31-32).

H ave you forgiven him yet?"

"How do you feel about him?"

These were the questions people asked the first days after Nathan was killed by a drunk driver. At the time, the easiest thing to say was, "I don't know how I

30

feel about him." I was trying to cope with Nate's death. I couldn't deal with the driver right then.

That answer got me through the first few weeks, but then I started asking myself the same questions. "How *do* I feel about him? *Have* I forgiven him?"

I was afraid to meet him face to face because I didn't know how I felt. What would I do when I had to see the man who killed my son, the man who had robbed us of the privilege of watching Nate grow up?

When I learned the accident had been caused by a drunk driver, anger overwhelmed me, but I remembered that I had those feelings of anger when Ethan died. At that time my anger wasn't directed toward a drunk driver—my anger was directed toward God. I felt I had been "done in" by God. I had trusted Him and told Him He could do His will in Ethan's life. Instead of healing Ethan, He had let him die.

My anger simmered into bitterness until I read a statement from Dr. S. I. McMillen's book, *None of These Diseases:*

> The moment I start hating a man, I become his slave. I can't work any more because he even controls my thoughts. My resentments produce too many stress hormones in my body and I become fatigued after only a few hours of work. The work I formerly enjoyed is now drudgery. . . .
>
> The man I hate hounds me wherever I go. I can't escape his tyrannical grasp on my mind.[1]

My anger and hatred hadn't been focused on a person, but on a situation. I was angry because Ethan was dead, and that anger was controlling me. After reading this I was able to confess my anger as sin and ask the Lord to help me be content in my situation.

When I learned Nathan had been killed by a drunk driver, those same feelings of anger and hatred welled up within me. I didn't want to be a slave to anger again, so I immediately asked God to remove those feelings and give me victory in the midst of this terrible situation. However, my prayer was not put to the test until the time I met the man who was responsible.

As I entered the second-floor hallway the first day we were to appear in court, I saw a man sitting in a wheelchair. I just knew he must be the one. As I walked closer to the wheelchair, it turned, and I saw the man's face. He looked like a very frightened man—not a killer at all. I didn't feel angry, nor did I want to scream or lash out at him—I just stood and let the tears fall. God had removed the bitterness and was allowing me to forgive this man.

Besides forgiveness, I also felt relief when I saw the man's face—relief that I was Nate's mother rather than his own mother. I sensed that this man's sin had caused his family deep heartache, and I was relieved that Nate had never brought us heartache, shame, or grief during all his seventeen years. We weren't having to help our child work through the guilt he would experience at causing someone else's death.

In the January 1985 issue of *Family Life Today*, Lewis Smedes identified four stages of forgiving:

> The first stage is hurt: When somebody causes you pain so deep and unfair that you cannot forget it, you are pushed into the first stage of the crisis of forgiving.
>
> The second stage is hate: You cannot shake the memory of how much you were hurt, and you cannot wish your enemy well. You sometimes want the person who hurt you to suffer as you are suffering.
>
> The third stage is healing: You are given

eyes to see the person who hurt you in a new light. Your memory is healed, you turn back the flow of pain and are free again.

The fourth stage is the coming together: You invite the person who hurt you back into your life; if he or she comes honestly, love can move you both toward a new and healed relationship.

The fourth stage depends on the person you forgive as much as it depends on you; sometimes he doesn't come back and you have to be healed alone.[2]

Nate died in February but I didn't see the driver of the other car until several months later. God needed that time to prepare my heart and get me ready to be forgiving.

I went through all of the stages Mr. Smedes mentioned. The hurt I felt seemed unbearable. Nate was gone. I would never see him on this earth again, and I was completely broken. A total stranger had caused us this relentless, throbbing pain and totally disrupted our lives.

Although I didn't actually hate the man, I hated the fact he could throw us into such chaos and still live as a free man, seemingly unscathed.

The summer after Nate's death, I was trying to locate a friend's home, and I got lost. I looked up at the street sign and realized I was on the street where the man lived who had killed Nate. I didn't want to be there, but before I could find a place to turn around, I saw him playing ball with his son.

After I turned the corner, I parked the car and cried. I hated it that he, the man who killed my son, could enjoy a summer afternoon with his son. He robbed me of a privilege he was still experiencing. Oh, how I wished he could feel my devastation and my sorrow.

The beginning of healing came when I met him in the

courtroom because I was able to see him in a new light, not only as the man who had come crashing into our lives, who had seemed to have little regard for our feelings, but I was able to see him also as a frightened, needy man.

Because of the legal circumstances, there has been no "coming together." I have experienced my healing alone. Although I have never been able to share my feelings with the man who caused Nate's death, God has healed me enough so that I am able to pray that God will bring him peace.

As Christians, we mistakenly expect all victims to be ready to offer instant forgiveness to those who have hurt them. A friend came to me the morning after Nathan died and asked me to go to the hospital to tell the driver of the other car I had forgiven him. In the middle of the night Glen and I had called the hospital chaplain, who is a friend of ours, and asked him to see the man as soon as possible, but I was not ready to meet him face to face.

Another acquaintance was so insistent I display forgiveness immediately, she sent a card to the man, signing our family's name along with hers, stating, "We love you and forgive you." I could have gone to the hospital immediately, or quickly sent a card proclaiming forgiveness, but in my case it would have been premature.

When we are grieving, we shouldn't feel compelled to rush forgiveness. It may be necessary to allow time for the situation to sink in and for God to do a work in our hearts. If you are the one who is grieving, be open to God's guiding and allow Him to lead you in the direction of forgiveness. I am not condoning vengeance or uncontrolled anger, but you may find there is a neutral stage where you have no feelings one way or the other; you are numb. The neutral stage can be a provision from God to protect you from feelings of grief or anger which would be too great for you to control. Forgiveness, especially in a traumatic or crisis situation, will take time. Give God time.

Although God helped me control feelings of bitterness and anger toward the drunk driver, I allowed myself to get tripped up in another area.

Because all of the teenagers in Nathan's car came from Christian families, I hoped we would be able to work together in harmony. However, we had difficulty agreeing about anything. Because of this, the insurance settlement, which we had hoped would happen in sixty to ninety days, took fifteen months—months of problems and hurt feelings. And my bitterness grew.

I knew God could help me overcome these feelings, but I didn't want His help. I preferred to sit and stew. Why couldn't the other families understand we needed to get all of the legal matters behind us? It was as though we were waiting for the benediction at the funeral. We couldn't make decisions on our own, and we couldn't control our schedule. Every time I thought I was beginning to learn to handle things, we would get a call from an attorney or the insurance company, and it would start all over again. I was angry at the situation and at the people who were "allowing everything to drag on so long."

When I saw the other families, my hands shook; and when they called, I cried. I was allowing my anger to dictate my reactions to everything and everyone around me. One day when the anger was boiling especially hot inside of me, I received a note from a friend. It said, "Marilyn, I don't understand everything that you're going through, but I have one thought I would like to share with you. 'Keep the wound clean.' "

What timing! I burst into tears as I cried out to God for help. I had not kept the wound clean but had allowed it to fester with so much bitterness. As I confessed my sin to the Lord, I asked Him to forgive me and help me

cleanse the wound of anything which would keep it from
healing properly: the anger, the bitterness, the frustration, the impatience. The desire for these attitudes to
leave came immediately, but it took, and still takes, lots
of work and determination to keep the festering from
beginning again. I have spent much time in study and
prayer, asking God to help me "keep the wound clean."

Joni Eareckson Tada's book *A Step Further* helped me
to look at our situation from others' points of view and
to learn to forgive others. Joni explains:

> It's a kind of scale, I finally reasoned. Every
> person alive fits somewhere onto a scale of
> suffering that ranges from little to much.
>
> And it's true. Wherever we happen to be on
> that scale—that is, however much suffering
> we have to endure—there are always those
> below us who suffer less, and those above
> who suffer more. The problem is we usually
> like to compare ourselves only with those who
> suffer less. That way we can pity ourselves
> and pretend we're at the top of the scale. But
> when we face reality and stand beside those
> who suffer more, our purple-heart medals
> don't shine so brightly.[3]

God let me see I had become pious about my suffering.
After all, how many people do you know who have
buried three children? I placed myself rather high on the
scale of suffering; surely no one had suffered more than
I had.

God rebuked me for my attitude and showed me many
people who had suffered more. At first I resisted the idea,
but I finally had to admit I didn't know what it was like
to be a Joni Eareckson, confined to a wheelchair for the
rest of my life, or to suffer through a divorce, or to sit by

the bed of a child who was in a coma. Many people were experiencing griefs at least equal to if not greater than mine.

I had to ask God to forgive me for my self-righteous attitudes and to help me show compassion toward those who are suffering whether or not their problems seem of great significance to me.

As I did this, God began to give me a greater compassion toward those with whom I had been angry. Perhaps they were experiencing the same thing I had experienced. From their position on the scale of suffering, they also might be having a hard time realizing that someone else could suffer more than they. I began to pray daily that God would supply their needs and give them peace and understanding. I prayed the same prayer for myself. A short time later, one of the families came to us and asked our forgiveness for their lack of understanding and compassion.

God does hear and answer our prayers, but many times the work has to begin with us. As I asked God to remove the roots of bitterness, He answered my prayer and replaced those bitter roots with roots of love and compassion.

God is kind in that He doesn't dump all of our faults on us at once. He knows how much we can handle at one time. God gave me the desire to forgive the drunk driver; then, many months later, He gently showed me that my attitude toward the other families was wrong and I obediently confessed my sin.

Nearly three years after Nate's death, I participated in a communion service with a small group of people. The leader suggested we ask God to show us any sin in our lives regarding the other people in the room, then with family members, and finally with others with whom we associated. As I prayed, I felt no problem with anyone in the group nor with my family, but as my thoughts moved on to others, God stopped me short.

I could hear the voice of the lady who told me, "Nate is dying because you have given up." I tried to reason, "But Lord, she's the one who needs forgiving; I didn't do anything wrong."

Instantly, God allowed me to see the bitterness that I had harbored against her. As I asked God to forgive me, a great load lifted from me, and then I was free to forgive my friend. God knew when I was able to deal with that sin and He did not confront me with it until that time.

If you have a friend who is struggling with forgiving someone, don't condemn him for his feelings. The best thing you can do is serve as a sounding board and pray him though the forgiving process.

If you are hurting because someone has caused you a deep and unfair pain and you have been pushed into the "crisis stage" of forgiving, give yourself time. Give God time. Your responsibility is to make sure you don't allow the wound to fester with anger and bitterness. Keep the wound clean. Stay open with God. He will lead you into forgiveness. As you offer the rose of forgiveness to someone else, you will receive your own rose, that great gift of freedom from the bondage of anger and bitterness.

The Rose of Remembrance

I thank my God upon every remembrance of you (Philippians 1:3).

G len and I frequently attend Compassionate Friends, a support group for bereaved parents. Each month, as newly bereaved parents come, they ask similar questions:

"Why don't people mention his name?"

"Why don't they talk about him?"

"Have they forgotten him already?"

Non-bereaved friends say, "We don't want to remind you of your loss or give you added grief, so it seems better not to talk about your child anymore."

In Joe Bayly's book, *The Last Thing We Talk About*, Mr.

Bayly writes that his little girl described her feelings about her brother's impending death as being "like something is pinned to the front of your mind all the time."[1]

Most people who have lost a loved one will agree with her. Everything else that goes into our mind has to be filtered through the thought, *My wife (or my husband or my child) is dead.* Rarely will you remind family members of something they are not already thinking about. You can be sure they will remember birthdays, the anniversaries of the death, and most assuredly the events that led up to the death.

One of my greatest dreads was the arrival of an anniversary of Nate's death when no one remembered. I realized my friends had been unusually faithful, but I knew there would undoubtedly come a time when I would not receive a card or a phone call on that very significant day. On the day of the eighth anniversary, I did not receive a card or a call from someone who had known Nate. (I did receive cards from them later in the week. But on the actual anniversary, none of their cards arrived.) However, I did receive two cards from people who had read my books and were wanting to thank me for what my books had meant to them as well as acknowledging the anniversary of Nate's death. What a beautiful aroma those special roses brought into my life that day!

The week of Nate's crash I had been very busy working on student aid applications, along with a national scholarship application which was due that week. As a counselor, I did those things the same month of each year. For two or three years after the accident I still got very depressed when I started working on those applications. It was as if I were heading toward the crash again, and it helped when people acknowledged that that time of year must be hard for me.

Some people say, "I don't want to mention it because I may cause you more hurt." I am going to hurt whether they mention it or not because I can't get away from reminders; they are all around me. When friends mention the anniversary date is coming up, they are reminding me of the accident, but they're also reminding me they are hurting with me. They're supporting me, and they care for me.

Although friends may mean well, their avoidance of talking about the one who has died can hurt the bereaved family deeply. I talk about Nate often because I enjoy talking about him. Acknowledging his existence helps keep him alive in my mind, and it is important to me to remember the normal, natural, human things about him.

From my loss of Jimmy and Ethan, I realize memories do fade. I didn't have either of those babies long enough to have many memories. Now, years later, I can barely picture their faces. When Nate died, I began to fear that in a few years I wouldn't be able to remember him clearly, so I asked for a special gift from the Lord. I prayed I would always be able to see an image in my mind of Nate alive, and I would be able to remember the sound of his voice. God granted my request in a unique way.

Shortly after the accident we learned Nate's coach had videotaped a basketball game less than two weeks before Nate died. On that tape, Nate is real. He directs traffic as he dribbles the ball down the court and he puts his arm around the coach as the coach gives him some new piece of strategy. I can see him pat another player on the back as he enters the game, and he even makes six points. Whenever I watch the tape, I still find myself cheering for him when he makes a good play. My memory of Nate alive is preserved forever on that tape.

More than two and a half years after Nate's death, I started to play a cassette tape of myself which I had recorded when I was speaking at a luncheon a few months earlier. I inadvertently placed the tape into the recorder on the wrong side. I listened to the woman speaking and thought, Who is that? That isn't my voice.

As I listened, I heard a piano and a male voice. I quickly realized I had discovered a tape of one of Nathan's voice lessons! I prayed, "Oh God, please let me hear him clearly; don't tease me with this." As he began to sing, the teacher suggested he move closer to her, which was also closer to the tape recorder. I could hear him perfectly. God answered my prayer!

I sat on the floor of our living room sobbing as I heard Nate sing one song and discuss it with his teacher. She asked, "Nate, do you have any more songs?"

He answered, "I've got one more. It isn't my favorite, but it's my mom's favorite and I want to learn it for her!"

I felt I had moved back in time, back to when things were normal, back when I couldn't comprehend how much emotional pain one body could stand. I hungrily devoured each precious note as Nate sang the beautiful, Jewish-sounding melody, "Pierce My Ear, O Lord."

When Nate finished, the teacher said, "Nate, that was beautiful. I understand why your mom likes that song."

In his typical phlegmatic fashion, Nate said, "Yeah, not much melody, but kind of mellow."

Can you possibly imagine the joy I felt as I listened to my Nate sing? It was like a special delivery letter from heaven. More than two years after Nate's death, God answered my request that I would never forget the sound of his voice.

Most people want to talk about their deceased loved one, they hunger for even small reminders, and they want you, as their friends, to help them keep the memory of that person alive. One bereaved parent stated, "A person's not dead until he's forgotten."

Obviously, this is an area where you must be sensitive. Let the bereaved person set the pace. If he changes the subject when you mention the deceased's name, he may be trying to tell you that it hurts too much right now to talk about his loss. Just follow his lead.

Nate was a cross-country runner. The fall after he died, many of his close friends were on the cross-country team at school. Christian, one of Nate's best friends, asked me to come and watch them run. I enjoyed the meet, but as the runners crossed the finish line, my mind flashed back to the previous year when Nate placed high enough to qualify for the league finals. A few tears slipped down my cheeks, but I wasn't embarrassed because I looked up and saw that Christian's father had tears in his eyes also. He came over, put his arm around me and said, "I'm thinking about him, too."

Many of Nate's friends wrote me notes with little stories about him. Sue, one of his classmates, wrote:

> One of the things that I continue to be thankful for is the precious memories I have of Nate. I miss walking through the halls and singing with Nate. He always had a song that he would share. He often asked me how he could help when no one else knew I was down. He carried my burdens. He was and is a dear friend. I just wanted you to share my thankfulness.

I dreaded the approach of June of 1984 because Nate would have graduated then. At baccalaureate the students presented a slide show of Nathan which they had compiled, with a tape of B. J. Thomas singing "Home Where I Belong" as background music. After the program they presented the slides and tape to me with this note:

Dear Mrs. Heavilin,
    This slide show in no way expressed all that

Nathan was to us or to you, but in a way, the words of the song, "Home Where I Belong," expressed our security in the fact that we will see Nate again.

We also pray that this little token of our love for Nate will continually remind you of our support for you and your family.

Nathan was an irreplaceable part of our class; but Nathan is home where he belongs.

With all our love in Him, the Class of 1984.

As a counselor, it was my job to present all of the scholarships and awards at the graduation ceremonies. I prayed God would dry up my seemingly never-ending well of tears as I prepared for that event.

Each year the seniors give roses to their parents during the ceremony. As a faculty member, I handed the roses to the students so they could take them to their parents. Many thoughts flooded my mind as I passed a flower to each student: *One of these should be mine. I wonder how Nate would give it to me. He would probably do something silly. He might be giggling.* Most of all, I was thinking, *I want a rose. I feel cheated and left out.*

After the students had returned to the platform, I saw two of the seniors walking toward me with a bouquet of roses and I was instantly overwhelmed! Their thoughtfulness assured me they cared for me and they missed Nate, too. God allowed me to see He was working in those teenagers' lives. He was making them more serious than most students would be on graduation night, and they were learning compassion through Nate's death.

Their action released both me and the audience to cry together. If I had fallen apart while making the scholarship presentations, I would have been crying alone in front of an audience. But their kind gesture made my loss public enough so that it was acceptable for us all to cry together. After a minute or so, we regained our composure and were able to proceed with the ceremony. Acknowledgment of my grief was very important to me because it gave me courage to go on.

Each year Glen and I attend the graduation to award the Nathan Heavilin Memorial Scholarship. I watch with much emotion as the graduates go out into the audience to give their parents a rose. I am now also able to watch with interest and anticipation because each year one of the graduates presents me with a rose. This quiet little tradition helps me know Nate is not forgotten and I'm sure it also serves as a reminder to all the parents of how fortunate they are as their children bring roses to them. And best of all, I get a very special hug from a teenager. How I cherish those hugs!

When others acknowledge that a situation might be hard, it often bolsters people to bravery. But when the bereaved are placed in a situation which is going to be difficult, and everyone goes on as if nothing has happened, it is much harder for them to keep their composure.

After people hear me share my story, they often ask, "How can you tell such a moving story without breaking down yourself? It seems everyone was crying except you."

I have learned that as long as the audience sheds tears at least occasionally while listening to my story, I can get through it without crying. However, if I ever spoke about the deaths of my three sons and it did not move the audience to tears, I know I would fall apart. Their tears say, "We're with you. We hurt for you." Their tears give me strength.

Another stress area will be the holidays. Families may need to give themselves permission not to celebrate holidays in the same way they did before their loved one died. After the death of their eighteen-year-old daughter, one family I knew went on a picnic for Thanksgiving and took a trip over the Christmas holidays. It is important for the family to talk together and be allowed to express their feelings freely about upcoming seasonal holidays, birthdays, and anniversaries.

If this is the case in your family, don't be hard on yourselves. The world is not going to stop if you don't celebrate Christmas this year. Some of your extended family may feel frustrated, but try to explain as kindly and gently as you can that your heart is just not ready for big celebrations yet.

Our family traditionally celebrated Christmas on Christmas Eve, and because that was also Aunt Lucille's birthday, we always made it a double celebration. But after Aunt Lucille and Uncle Louie, Mom's sister and brother-in-law, died as a result of the explosion and flash fire, Mom wanted to cancel December, too. However, Christmas continued to come.

A friend of my mother's sent her a poem that expressed all our feelings. My mom put the poem in with a box of pictures and tucked it away. The December after Nate's death I was sorting through that box and found the poem. What timing! Once again Christmas, a birthday, and the loss of a loved one were all mixed together. The poem was appropriate, even thirty-four years later, so I made copies of it and sent it to other bereaved friends.

"Merry" Christmas

I question if Christmas can ever be "merry,"
Except to the heart of an innocent child —
For when time has taught us the meaning of sorrow
And sobered the spirits that once were so wild,

When all the green graves that lie scattered behind us
Like milestones are marking the length of the way,
And echoes of voices that no more shall greet us
Have saddened the chimes of the bright
Christmas Day—

We may not be merry, the long years forbid it,
The years that have brought us such manifold smarts,
But we may be happy, if only we carry
The Spirit of Christmas deep down in our hearts.

Hence I shall not wish you the old "Merry Christmas,"
since that is of shadowless childhood a part,
But one that is holy and happy and peaceful,
The Spirit of Christmas deep down in your heart.

- Author unknown

This can be a time to make some new memories and establish new traditions. It was four years after Nathan's death before I could do much Christmas decorating or have a real tree. That Christmas, Glen and I went out and cut down the biggest tree we could find. Since we had recently bought and refurbished a seventy-five-year-old Victorian house, I made many new decorations for our Christmas tree and did everything I could think of to use the Victorian theme all through the holidays. To celebrate, Glen and I invited friends to go Christmas caroling with us. Several women friends joined me one afternoon for a Victorian tea and a brief piano and violin recital provided by one of my friends. These events took planning and effort on my part, and it wasn't always easy. Yet as we build new memories, we will become more confident that we can face the holidays and the future without our loved one.

Over the past few years I have collected rose motif Christmas ornaments for our tree. Each piece has a story;

who gave it to me or where I purchased it. The rose theme gives me an opportunity to explain to my guests the significance of roses to me. I also had a florist design a Christmas centerpiece which includes three silk roses and three candles which we light for each special event during the Christmas season.

Often after the death of a child or spouse, adults would be quite content to ignore the holidays, but they are forced to face traditional celebrations because of other children in the family. Friends can help in these situations by offering to take the children Christmas shopping, or to visit Santa Claus.

One family told me how they spent their first Christmas afternoon assembling a memory book of their deceased child. There were tears, of course, but they also spent a lot of time laughing as the pictures and notes brought back thoughts of the wonderful times they had had together. A family activity like this can help the children approach grieving in a healthy way.

It is important also for us to be sensitive when choosing Christmas cards for the recently bereaved. I was so relieved when I opened one envelope and read a card that said, "To Comfort You at Christmas." What a contrast to all of the jolly "Ho, Ho, Ho" cards that arrived in each day's mail. Writing a note to the bereaved family acknowledging that this holiday may be difficult and perhaps including a positive statement or story about the deceased will be appreciated.

My daughter and her husband did something very special to help us through our first Christmas after Nate died. Since Nate's birthday was Christmas Day, I was apprehensive about it all. I invited many of our friends to spend the day with us and I claimed the promise I had discovered many months before that God would give us "roses in December."

Christmas morning, my son-in-law Mike showed me a

card he had placed on the Christmas tree. It was addressed to Nate, but Mike handed it to me.

Dear Family,

Mellyn and I wanted to do something special this Christmas in thanksgiving to our Father for His incredible blessings upon us.

It is our desire, if the Lord wills, to establish a tradition of Christmastime giving—a real sacrifice of ourselves for others, in memory of Nathan.

Mike and Mellyn

The first year they took a basket of food to a needy family and told the family they were doing this in memory of their brother Nathan. This past year, they helped a Vietnamese family. A remembrance like that is a very special rose in December.

We have adopted the same custom. For several years at Christmas we chose a boy to send to basketball camp in memory of Nate. I have also bought clothes for a child at the Children's Home Society and asked specifically that they be given to a teenage boy. One year, our friends Nancy and Peter sent a contribution to a Christian organization in Nate's name.

I am thankful for the friends who have stuck with us during these difficult years. Undoubtedly there were times when they were tired of hearing about Nate, the accident, the trial, the insurance, etc. They probably wondered if we would ever stop talking about him, but they were patient and they let us talk. It was a very important part of our healing.

We don't talk about Nate constantly now. We are

beginning to see him as "one of the children," not necessarily just as the "one who died."

Our friends have learned to talk about him in a natural way, too. We can laugh about his funny and sometimes irritating habits, the times he did something wrong, his pet peeves, and all of the fun we had with him. He is beginning to take a normal spot in the history of the Heavilin family. Much of this normality has been regained because our friends have given us freedom to talk and work through our loss. They have also taken time to remember with us, for which we will be forever grateful.

If you have experienced a recent loss, let me encourage you to find friends with whom you can talk freely. Support groups can be helpful also. Perhaps there is a group in your church that can meet your needs. If not, try to find a group such as Compassionate Friends. Although they do not have a Christian emphasis, you will find people there who will understand your feelings and your frustrations.

If you have friends or coworkers with whom you feel strained because you can't share how you really feel, don't be too hard on them. If they are close friends, gently explain your needs. If they still don't respond, try to understand that their background and training may not free them to be as open as you would like them to be. Love them anyway, and let them learn from you. Perhaps they will observe enough so that they will be able to pass your attitudes on to others even if they can't help you. Thank God for all of the friends He gives you who do understand. They are beautiful, priceless roses.

The Rose of Friendship

A true friend is always loyal, and a brother is born to help in time of need (Proverbs 17:17 TLB).

When I was a little girl, my father had a plaque hanging in his office which read, "He is rich who has two friends." After Nathan's death, God showed me that regarding friends, I was a millionaire! Most people going through a tragedy have more help than they need the first week or so. But soon the crowd thins out. The bereaved often ask, "Where are all those people who said they would help me?"

I was afraid that would happen in our case, but it didn't. Oh, of course, the crowd thinned out, but we had many people who stuck with us. When Nate died, my friend Donna Lynn was expecting her sixth child. She didn't have a lot of time to come to my house or take me to lunch, but her limited time didn't keep her from helping. She helped by letting me help her. She would call and say, "Marilyn, I need some typing done [or someone to watch the baby, or someone to be outside with her four-year-old]. Will you come and help me?"

After I helped her, we would have some time to talk. Donna Lynn accomplished two things with this approach. She helped me feel useful again and showed she cared by spending quality time with me. I'm glad she didn't let her busy schedule get in the way of helping a friend.

I didn't know Joan well before the accident, although her children were close friends of Nate's. That didn't stop her from coming to our house the very first morning and cooking breakfast for us. A few weeks later at church, Joan said, "Marilyn, I just want to tell you how much I appreciate it that you're letting the people in this church watch you grieve. You are open about how we can help you. You aren't trying to hide your feelings from us. We're a new church, and we need to learn how to work with people in crisis."

Then she went on to ask, "Would you be willing to meet me for lunch periodically so I can learn more from you?"

Her psychology was wonderful. She could have said, "Let me take you to lunch so that I can help you, honey." But she didn't. She put me in a position where I felt comfortable accepting her invitation. She didn't make me feel like a charity case.

When I accepted her offer, I had no idea of all we would be facing in the next few months. Many times I got so frustrated with the legal system, or the insurance situation, that I would think to myself, *If I can just hang on until Wednesday when I have lunch with Joan, I'll be okay.*

I knew I could be honest with Joan. I didn't have to be guarded about what I said. I could trust her with my deepest feelings. Through those very difficult months, Joan was my release valve. She helped me keep my sanity and a proper perspective on the situation.

During one of those lunches, Joan shared how Nate's death had affected her family. Her daughters Sue and Donna were so moved by his death that just going to the funeral, paying their respects, and helping us didn't seem like enough. As a family, they decided to do something that would involve them personally. For several weeks their family had a moratorium on television in memory of Nate. They felt if the whole country could do so in honor of a deceased president, the Morrill family could certainly curtail their television watching in honor of a friend. Their act of sacrifice was very kind, but it meant even more because they shared it with us. The bereaved are encouraged when they know their loss is shared by others.

My friend Nancy was the first person we called after we heard about the accident. She came to the hospital immediately—a thermos of coffee in hand—and then came home with us and stayed until midnight Friday evening. Nancy and her husband, Pete, practically lived with us for the next two or three weeks.

Nancy made all of the phone calls we couldn't make; she helped arrange for food to be brought in; and she took care of our guests. Pete handled the logistics of such things as getting people from one place to another and bringing chairs from the church to our house after the funeral.

A few weeks later I discovered Nancy had done something even more special as she handed me a legal-sized notepad and a cassette tape. She said, "Here's the start of your book whenever you decide to write about this."

She went on to explain that she had been taking notes

for the past few weeks about everything that had been going on at our house: the people, the phone calls, the gifts, the cards, and our reactions. Then she had made a tape of her personal feelings about Nate's death.

It was a long time before I could listen to the tape, and it was hard to imagine I would ever forget the details of those two weeks. But as I read the notes and listened to the tape about six months later, I discovered I had already forgotten much of what had happened. As time passes, I realize more and more how special Nancy's gift really was.

The best thing some of my friends did for me was just to let me cry. Sometimes, the minute I would hear a friend's voice, I would start to cry. My friends didn't condemn me; they simply let me express my emotions.

My friend Diana is very sensitive to my needs, and she can tell when I am getting ready for a good cry. When I call and ask if she can meet me at my favorite restaurant for a piece of pie, she doesn't question me. She just says, "What time?" It is so comfortable to be with Diana because she freely admits she misses Nate, too. She doesn't just watch me cry; she cries with me. That's a true friend.

On the second anniversary of Nate's home-going, my mother took flowers to the grave. She found a bouquet already there with a card that read, "Nate, we'll never forget you. See you later."

It was from Diana and her family. Diana is a special rose in our bouquet of December roses.

Friends can be sensitive to the needs of children in bereaved families by giving them extra attention, taking them places, or just listening to them. Frequently, the parents are so distraught themselves they are oblivious to the needs of the children.

Our son Matt had sat with his friend Roger the November before Nate's death when Roger's wife faced serious surgery. He carried food to Roger, ran errands for him, and was his sounding board.

After Nate's crash, Roger was able to return the favor to Matt. He came to the hospital and then stuck with Matt during the remainder of the day.

In Matt's words, Nate had been his "social life" for several years. He had transported Nate and his friends to many high school events and even had driven them on the field trip to Los Angeles the day of the accident. Roger recognized the empty space that Matt would need to fill and he helped by spending as much time with him as possible in the early weeks following the accident. Often bereaved brothers and sisters are forgotten, so we are grateful that Roger saw he could minister to Matt just by being there.

Our pastor was a special friend to us. Pastors often want to spend time with bereaved families, but their schedules won't allow for daily or weekly calls, and the families seem to get lost in the pool of good intentions. Our pastor found a way to keep in touch with us without spending a lot of time. The greatest thing he did was come as soon as we called. The week of the funeral he stopped by daily, but after that he called us each evening between nine and ten. We both got on the phone for a three-way conversation with him which enabled us to hear each other's reaction to his questions.

He would ask, "How did it go today?" We would relate the happenings of the day. "How do you feel about today's happenings?" Sometimes we felt good, and sometimes we didn't. Often we would shed a few tears with him.

"What's happening tomorrow?" We would relate our plans; perhaps we had a special meeting or a court date.

"Let's pray." We would join in conversational prayer for the events of the next day.

"Now go to bed and get some rest." Often we went to

bed simply because he suggested it. Sometimes we didn't seem able to make even those simple decisions for ourselves. Those conversations usually took only five to ten minutes, but they met a vital need in our lives. The pastor communicated that he cared, and he also sensed if we had some special needs the church could meet.

In a large church, the pastor probably would not be able to make contact through a daily phone call, but he could assign an elder, deacon, deaconess, or another caring person to keep in touch with the family and serve as a link to himself and to the church.

A pastor's secretary could keep a card file, with notations such as: "Nate Heavilin died February 10, 1983; send Glen and Marilyn a card." This special touch would be greatly appreciated by the bereaved family.

Occasionally during the next few months a note would appear in our bulletin, "Remember to pray for the Heavilins as they continue to adjust to their recent loss." Our pastor was giving us time to grieve.

I sent a survey to about forty families I have met over the past few years who have experienced the loss of a family member. I asked them to score their treatment by medical personnel, clergy, morticians, law enforcement agents, and lawyers. Along with medical personnel, the clergy got the lowest marks. Many of the families felt the clergy were unwilling to spend time with them and unable to answer their questions. Most commented that they seldom saw the clergy again after the funeral.

One friend related that about a month after his son's death, the pastor did call and ask, "How are you doing?"

Ben thought, finally someone is interested in us, so he took the risk of answering honestly and said, "Well, Pastor, we're really not doing very well. My wife and I are having trouble talking to each other, and I'm depressed most of the time."

There was silence. Finally Ben realized that the pastor

couldn't handle his openness, so he pulled the mask of peace back over his heart and said, "Oh, really, Pastor, I'm just having a bad day. All in all, we're doing just fine."

The pastor muttered, "Well, I'm glad to hear that," and quickly ended the call.

Why would a pastor do something like that? First, because he has not been prepared to deal with the bereaved. Few seminaries deal with the subject of death except to teach future pastors how to conduct a funeral. Second, often when we are open with him and try to describe the hurt inside of us, he thinks we expect him to have a quick fix. Since he doesn't have a way to patch us up and take the pain away, he feels uncomfortable around us and finds it easier to stay away. When we say we're doing "just fine," he feels better and doesn't feel obligated to meet our needs.

Few of the bereaved are looking for a quick fix. It doesn't take us long to realize that our problem can't be taken care of quickly and we don't really expect anyone to fix it. What we do need is knowledgeable people around us who will listen and at least discuss our questions with us.

Pastors should be well versed on what their particular denomination teaches on the subjects of heaven, hell, and salvation. What is heaven like? Is my loved one there? What happens to babies when they die? If my loved one committed suicide or a terrible crime before he died, can he still go to heaven? Will we know each other in heaven? What part did God play in all of this?

Most bereaved people will appreciate a pastor who has thought through these issues and has come to some conclusions and is willing to interact with his parishioners on these topics. Even a well-thought-out "I don't know" will be accepted.

I have spent a lot of time thinking about the sovereignty of God in the past few years. I have searched the

Scriptures and formed what I hope are biblically based opinions on the subject. However, when I have wanted to bounce my ideas off someone else, I have had difficulty finding clergy who were willing to interact with me. I am very grateful to one pastor friend who has been willing to listen to me and read my writings to make sure I'm still on track. He hasn't judged me when my theories have seemed strange or out in left field; he has just patiently guided me toward what the Bible says.

When a loved one dies, even the unchurched and most non-religious people will start thinking about heaven and a life after death. It behooves pastors and churched people to be ready with some well-documented answers. Although people want to help the bereaved, many times they don't because they simply don't know what to do. We had to be willing to make our needs known. Sometimes this was hard because we didn't want to admit we needed other people. But when we did, we found most people willing and even anxious to help us.

There were days when the depression was so heavy I didn't have the strength to pick up the phone and call so someone could encourage me. On those days, I cried out to God and said, "God, I think I need help. If You agree with me, please have someone call me or contact me because I just don't have the strength to reach out to anyone today. If no one calls, then I'll know that You want me to work through this alone with You. I will trust You to meet my needs in the right way."

My prayer has always been answered, and I have received many calls from people stating, "I don't know why I'm calling, but God just keeps bringing you to my mind, so I had to call to see how you're doing."

Other times I didn't receive any calls, but God would show me a Scripture or lead me to a book, or give me a special thought that would lift my spirits and help me go on with life.

My friend Irene lives in Chicago, more than two thousand miles away, but she and I have become very sensitive to each other's needs.

One day I felt a strong desire to call Irene. I tried several times, but no one was home. When I finally reached her late that evening, Irene heard my voice and burst into tears. She sobbed, "Oh Marilyn, Jonathan [her only child] is in the hospital and we don't know what's wrong with him."

After Irene shared more details with me, we were able to pray together and claim God's peace for Irene, Jonathan, and the rest of the family. Irene received comfort in the realization that if God cared enough about her to touch the heart of a friend thousands of miles away, then surely He was aware of Jonathan's needs and would care for him, too, which He did.

When God puts someone on your mind, respond right away. God is most likely wanting to use you to respond to that person's immediate need. If you can't call or visit, then at least take time to pray, asking God to meet his or her needs as He sees fit.

A friend will not force himself on those in need, but will be responsive to their needs. A faithful friend is a beautiful rose.

If you are the bereaved person, be willing to let your needs be known. When you're having a terrible day, don't be afraid to admit it. Call somebody and just say, "Help." If you are so discouraged you don't have the strength to ask for help from other people, remember God has promised He will always be with you.

"The LORD is nigh unto them that are of a broken heart; and saveth such as be of a contrite spirit" (Ps. 34:18). Call on Him. He will hear, and He will answer. He wants to be your forever friend.

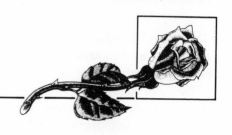

The Rose
of
Understanding

How much better is wisdom than gold, and understanding than silver! (Proverbs 16:16 TLB)

W hen Nathan died, I felt compelled to get back immediately into my regular routines at work, at home, and in my social life. It seemed that continuing on in all of my previous patterns could shut out the fact he was gone, as if his death were a dream or a mistake. I thought repeating normal patterns would make me feel normal again.

So, less than two weeks after Nate died, I returned to

my job at the high school where he had attended. The trip to school, Nate's and my private time together, had always been so much fun. Now, making the drive alone was horrible. I tried to listen to tapes, but I couldn't retain what I heard. The traffic made me nervous, and I felt nauseated as I drove past the wrecking lot where Nate's crushed car was stored.

Being at school seemed so strange: I had lost track of my purpose for being there. I walked into my office and all I could see was the chair where Nate sat each morning. Since teachers had to arrive early, Nate usually studied in my office before school started. As I would look into my room from the doorway after the teachers' meeting, I could see this lanky boy, sprawled comfortably in a chair, his size-eleven feet propped on another chair. When I returned to work, that scene, still vivid in my mind, haunted me.

The first day back, I learned that two of my students had received highly coveted scholarships, the very ones I had worked on so enthusiastically the day of Nate's accident. Upon hearing they had won, I burst into uncontrollable sobbing. Two weeks earlier I would have been elated; of course, I was still happy for them, but my heart was breaking because as his counselor I would never get a chance to help my Nate win a scholarship. After two hours of trying to work, I went home.

Occasionally I tried to write my feelings:

> The fog still hasn't lifted. I move, I walk, I talk, but it is all automatic. There is little feeling. Sometimes the fog lifts and the feelings rush in. Then, all I can do is cry. It seems the only time I am real, reacting honestly, without guarding every word or look, I start to cry. When the fog lifts for a brief moment, it's as though someone just kicked me in the stom-

ach. As I am reeling with the pain, my mind
registers the one prevailing thought: Nathan
is gone; *Nathan is gone.* When I can't stand the
pain anymore, my mind goes back into neutral, back into the fog.

Although I managed to continue working for the next
two years, time didn't really improve the situation. Often
I felt I was stumbling around in a dream; my mind
wouldn't concentrate on any one thing for more than a
few minutes. The extracurricular activities—basketball,
cross-country, ensemble—lost their meaning. There were
constant reminders everywhere—scholarships, graduation, homecoming. Within a few weeks everyone else
was back to normal, but Glen and I finally realized we
had no normal to get back to. We had to learn a new
normal, a normal without Nate.

Society needs to understand what trauma is and what
it (especially an unexpected loss) does to a person. We
may look all right on the outside, but our minds do not
function properly, and may not for months or even years.
I related to a young mother who had just lost a six-week-
old child how sometimes I could not keep a thought in
my head long enough to find a piece of paper and write
it down. She exclaimed, "Oh, thank goodness you have
that problem, too. I thought I was losing my mind!"

Parents at Compassionate Friends have shared that
sometimes they are driving on the freeway and they can't
remember where they're going. Others have called someone and when the person answers, they can't remember
whom they were calling. Many bereaved people change
educational or vocational plans because they have lost
the drive to go on in the same direction. These situations
often don't improve in the first few months; it may be
years before the person can remain constant in his lifestyle.

It helps if pastors, counselors, and friends understand that these reactions are normal. They can encourage the bereaved person not to give up but to try to discover if a temporary adjustment can be made. An extended leave of absence, a day off each week, or even a change to a part-time position may relieve the immediate pressure. Above all, they should help the bereaved person understand he should not feel guilty about being unable to function normally. The situation isn't normal after a death or other severe crisis, and it's okay to try to make things easier until life becomes more stable.

It's not unusual for people in crisis to feel they're in spiritual limbo. Even mature Christians may not have the mental strength to maintain normal Christian patterns.

When their only child, Robert, was killed in an automobile accident, Dick and Delores displayed amazing strength. The memorial service was honoring to the Lord and many lives were touched through it. But Delores recalls, "For three weeks after Robert's death I couldn't pray for myself but felt the power of others praying for me. After this period, I had a particularly bad day and was unable to cope. Then I realized that no one was praying, and God revealed to me that I now needed to express my own needs directly to Him."

The grief process takes a different path for each person, but it is important that he allow himself to grieve. No one who has lost a loved one is going to get a special reward in heaven for returning to normalcy immediately as though the person never existed. Those who handle a loss well are usually those who acknowledge their pain, admit to feelings of anger or bitterness, work through those feelings, and give themselves time to heal.

My friend Barbara discovered the importance of allowing herself to grieve through two loss experiences. She says:

At the time our son was stillborn at full term,

we were living out in the country without a single house in sight. We were relatively new in the community and, though we were attending church occasionally, our roots were not deep. The church was also without a pastor.

Our son was born in the same hospital and ward where I had been working as a nurse only weeks earlier so the nurses were my co-workers. A woman from our church also delivered the same day and she and her healthy baby were across the hall. None of our family lived close by.

As I look back, I realize I was still playing the role of nurse—being concerned for everyone else's feelings and stuffing my own. I even helped the staff with their charting and so everyone felt I was doing "just great." No one visited us and my husband and the funeral director attended the baby's funeral all alone. My tears (and there were many) were saved for when the door was closed and it was safe—like at night when the staff was scarce and people thought I was sleeping.

Our families never discussed our loss. It was as though I had never even had a baby. My husband was extremely pleasant and kind but after a couple of weeks he too felt it was time to move on with life—and as a result those wounds never really healed.

It wasn't until twenty-three years later and the fire in which our house burned that I really understood the grieving process, and then quite by accident. We lost everything, including our dog. Since the fire was considered a disaster and many of our friends also lost their homes or came close to losing them, people wanted to talk. We had calls from all over the United States and many friends stopped by to visit and wanted to hear everything. At first I cried lots as they probed, but then it became easier and easier to handle and before long I realized that those wounds had healed well. It was okay to weep.

I also became aware of the reasons healing had not occurred those many years earlier. No one deliberately wanted to hurt us. It is just so difficult to probe and see someone struggle and keep probing. However, it is essential if healing is to occur.

Apparently people are more comfortable probing about things (such as fires) as opposed to the loss of a person, and I still struggle with that.

Another difficult step for some in the healing process is cleaning out the deceased person's room and distributing his possessions. There is no particular time after the death when it is best to do this, but I can tell you what was comfortable for me.

As I mentioned in the first chapter, when Jimmy died some well-meaning friends emptied our house of all reminders of Jimmy the very first day while I was out of the house, without my knowledge or consent. I came home to discover an empty bedroom and I was enraged. I managed to conceal my feelings because I realized my friends had not intended to hurt me, but I felt they had trodden on sacred ground. I needed to take care of Jimmy's things as a part of my grief work, and I needed to do it when it was comfortable for me.

When Nate died, the very next morning I knew that his new Nikes and his golf clubs should go to his brother-in-

law, Mike. A stuffed musical dog from his childhood
went to his girlfriend, Sheila, and his gold monogram key
ring went to Matt after we had it especially engraved on
the back, "To a super brother."

A few weeks later I asked some of Nate's closest friends
to come over and go through his closet and choose any
clothing they would like. I gave some things to a cousin
for her son and sent the remaining clothes to Goodwill. I
saved Nate's sweatsuit and a cowboy suit I had made for
him when he was eight—they are for our grandchildren.

It was several months before I could go through his
drawers, desk, and notebooks. When the time came, I
asked Mellyn to spend the day with me and help finish
this heartrending project. How or when you tackle this
difficult assignment is up to you, but I would recommend
you not try it alone. Find someone who shares your grief
and can understand and share your memories and your
tears.

As the friend of a grieving person, you may be able to
identify stress points before he can. Let him know that it
is all right to back away and say, "I've had enough."
That's not admitting defeat; it's using good sense. Often
the grieving person cannot step outside of the situation
enough to recognize when he's pushing himself too far.

My son Matt met a need in my life with a solution I
didn't really appreciate at the time. He noticed I had
difficulty with some of the phone calls I received—such
as the lady who called to tell me what a nice man the
drunk driver was and how much he liked children, or the
agent from the loan company who called to make sure
we were going to make the final payment on our mangled
Toyota, but never bothered to offer his condolences—so
Matt bought me a telephone answering machine.

I had always hated those things. I found it irritating
when I called someone only to have a little machine talk
back to me. However, I knew Matt had done the right

thing. Some days I wasn't up to talking to anyone, and I always seemed to have difficulty talking to the families of the other young people who had been in the accident or to anyone regarding the legal matters, so I decided to try the answering machine. Just knowing who was calling before I decided if I wanted to answer the phone was a great relief to me. Matt helped me in a situation where I seemed unable to help myself because I felt an obligation always to be available to others.

When you are hurting, it takes a lot of effort to try to help yourself, but the effort is worth it. Whether your new venture is traveling, joining a special interest group, or starting a project, although it won't take the hurt away, it will get you into the mainstream of life again, and slowly the hurt will become more bearable.

It is important to understand that the bereaved may be in shock for a few days or a few months; they need to grieve; and they may have trouble in their jobs and in their families. The rose of understanding is one we all can acquire by being observant, listening to the bereaved, and responding to what we observe.

The interests or activities that help a bereaved person deal with his grief may seem strange to someone else; however, I believe bereaved people can do some rather unusual things and still be operating within the realm of normal. But I'm sure some of you are asking, "How can we tell if someone has moved outside the 'normal' limits?"

I am not a doctor or a psychologist so I can only share with you the observations of a layperson who has experienced a great deal of grief and has talked with many people who are grieving.

If a person refuses to acknowledge that someone is dead, keeps talking in the past, or continually seems to get the past and the present confused, I believe he needs professional help. If he becomes reclusive or deeply depressed, or if he openly talks of suicide, he should begin seeing a counselor.

I am reluctant to put timelines on grief because the healing process takes different lengths of time with each person, but you should be able to observe constant improvement. Even though improvement seems to come more slowly than you would like, if there is consistent progress, the person is probably doing all right.

However, the healing might be accelerated if the person were to talk with a counselor or join a support group. Christians often hesitate to seek professional help, feeling they shouldn't need it. But frequently that is exactly what they do need. It is important to get referrals and to choose a counselor carefully. If you are the grieving person, you should call the counseling center and inquire whether they have counselors who deal specifically with grief therapy before you make an appointment. Although Glen and I did not seek professional counseling, we did find great help through Compassionate Friends, a support group for bereaved parents. This statement appeared in one of their recent newsletters:

> Our grief as parents of dead children is totally unique. Not even other bereaved parents can completely understand our grief. We are all individuals and we therefore grieve in our own very personal way. What we do have in common, though, is our loss. And that loss, no matter by what means, is very overwhelming. By our coming together we are able to share our pain and to come to the sad realization that we are not alone. At our meetings we discover other parents whose child died by similar circumstances.This will not erase our pain, but will help to support us.

In many areas there are support groups for people who have suffered specific types of losses, such as widows, widowers, families of suicide victims, and those whose children have died from Sudden Infant Death Syndrome. If you cannot find a group in your area, you may want to start one. Ask your pastor or the local funeral director for names of people who have had recent losses similar to yours. Call and invite them to have lunch with you or meet at your home for coffee. You very likely will find comfort in sharing your experiences and feelings with each other. You will be strengthened just by realizing you were able to help a fellow griever.

When you have experienced the death of someone close, or a divorce, or some other life-changing trauma, realize that your mind, body, and emotions have to adjust to this change. Read helpful books, tell others how you feel, make adjustments in your lifestyle to ease the stress, and ask God to help you learn valuable truths you can share with others, so you, too, can be a beautiful rose of understanding to those around you.

The Rose
of
Innocence

But whoso shall offend one of these little ones which believe in me, it were better for him that a millstone were hanged about his neck, and that he were drowned in the depth of the sea (Matthew 18:6).

When a crisis comes, as adults we tend to get involved in dealing with our own grief, and many times the children in the family are put in the care of a close friend or relative until "things have returned to normal." Whether children attend the funeral or not, it is important for someone to be available to answer their questions and meet their needs.

When our Jimmy died of crib death in 1964, our daughter Mellyn was almost three years old. Jimmy's crib was in Mellyn's room. Glen went in to check on the children and discovered the baby was dead. For the next few minutes our attention was focused on Jimmy. Finally, I realized that Mellyn was still in the room, huddled against the wall on her bed. Her first words were, "I didn't hurt Jimmy."

I assured her I knew she had done nothing wrong and told her an angel had taken Jimmy to heaven to be with Jesus. Months later I awoke in the night aware of a little hand moving across my face. Mellyn looked so relieved when she saw me move, and she said, "I just wanted to see if God took you, too." Words that had been comforting to me had been discomfiting to a three-year-old.

After Jimmy's death, Mellyn reverted to baby talk and many babyish mannerisms. She often climbed up on my lap and said, "I'll be your baby now." It was two or three years before we felt Mellyn was a relaxed, carefree little girl again.

My brother was only two when his parents died and my parents adopted him. He can't really remember his birth parents nor the events surrounding the tragedy, but for many months afterward he would scream with fear when my mother left him with anyone else. He may not have been able to remember what had happened, but he definitely remembered the feelings of fear when his mommy and daddy left and never came back.

A pamphlet distributed by Mothers Against Drunk Drivers (MADD) states:

> A child of two can sense loss and suffer the feelings that go with loss, but he cannot understand what death is. The child will pick up

on the grief and anxiety in his surroundings and will need touching or holding. Explanations, however, will not be understood. The child this young can only understand that someone is present or not present.

What one does is far more important to the child this young than what one says. Generally, it is best done with large doses of tender loving care—holding, cuddling, and stroking.

A child between the ages of four and six may talk of the death of the person in the same detached way that he may talk of the death of a pet. This may be disturbing to the adults around him and their reaction may be confusing. Crying may be more out of confusion about what others are experiencing rather than the death itself.

Most commonly, seven- or eight-year-olds become fearful of death because they realize for the first time that it is real. . . . Some of their questions may indicate fears of their own death. Death can now be seen as an attacker who takes life. Although able to accept the finality of death, many of the factors of early childhood still apply. It is important for children of this age to express their sadness, anger, fear, and guilt.[1]

Mellyn was four-and-a-half when Ethan died and I was very concerned about how she would react since Jimmy's death had been so difficult for her. However, she surprised us all. When she was told of Ethan's death, she commented, "That's okay, I've still got Nathan!"

When my grandmother died just two months later, Mellyn heard me say how bad I felt because Grandma never got to see Nathan. She asked, "Is Grandma in heaven?"

When I said yes, she concluded, "Well, Ethan was Nate's identical twin, so he looks just like Nate. If Grandma's in heaven, she has seen Ethan, so she knows what Nate looks like."

She played with her toys a few minutes and then asked, "Do you have another grandma in heaven?"

I said, "Yes, my Grandma Empey."

With the beautifully innocent faith of a little child, Mellyn said, "Then she can have Jimmy."

Through Mellyn's faith she allowed me to see a picture of two grandmas rocking their great-grandchildren in heaven.

I personally feel it is good for children to be involved with as much of the grief experience as they are comfortable with, but it should not be forced. One family I know has experienced the deaths of three immediate family members in the past year. After the third death, their ten-year-old child said, "I can't go to another funeral," and the parents made the wise decision to let her stay home.

When a child dies, the siblings may feel guilty because God didn't take them instead of their brother or sister since, from their point of view, he or she was the smart one or the cute one, or Mom or Dad liked him or her better. A younger child may try to take the place of an older child by assuming his responsibilities, moving into his room, or wearing his clothes.

Parents need to assure this child that they like him just as he is and they don't want him to be an imitation of someone else. Young people also may take undeserved responsibility for the death. I met a young boy whose sister committed suicide. When the sister had attempted suicide previously, the brother had determined he was going to stay with her and watch her so that she could never try suicide again. However, one day when the boy had to leave the house for a legitimate reason, the sister took the opportunity to kill herself. My young friend was filled with self-imposed guilt, "If I had just made her go with me, this would not have happened."

The parents' reassurance was not enough in this case. The boy needed an outsider's perspective to help him work through his grief and be able to forgive himself before he could realize his sister's death was not his fault.

Sometimes the remaining child will display anger because his life has been disrupted or because all of the attention seems to be focused on the dead instead of on the living. He may need help in getting the right assessment of his own importance. We also need to be careful how we talk about the deceased child. We may tend to talk only about his good qualities and not acknowledge his faults to the point that the remaining children begin to feel inferior and less important than the absent child. Being aware of this potential problem can help us avoid it.

When my aunt and uncle were fatally injured in a gas stove explosion, I was twelve. My parents considered leaving me with a babysitter while they drove to the hospital in northern Michigan, but I begged them to take me along. I did not want to be separated from my family. If we were facing trouble, I wanted us to face it together.

We arrived at the motel late in the evening and my grandparents filled us in on the details of the accident. Grandpa took my parents to the hospital and I crawled into bed with Grandma. It was the middle of the night when Grandpa walked in and said, "Louie's dead!" I can still feel my Grandma's tears falling on me as we sat on the edge of the bed and she held me so tightly.

Early the next morning we all went to the hospital to sit with my Aunt Lucille. Everyone was allowed to go into her room except me because I was not old enough, so I sat in the waiting room alone most of the day. Frequently my father came out to give me a report. One report was: "Lucille is now unconscious; we don't think she'll live much longer." Later that afternoon, Lucille died.

When the family went to see Lucille's children in the burn ward, the doctor said I could not go. I started to cry and said, "Are they dying, too?" My mother finally convinced the doctor I needed to see the children and know they were all right. My fears were relieved when I was able to talk with the children. I am thankful my parents were honest with me but I am also glad they sensed my emotional need to see the children.

During the week of the funeral people came to the house to talk with my mom and dad and my grandparents, but I don't remember anyone talking specifically with me. When I returned to school, my teacher came up to me, put her arms around me, and asked me how I was doing. The tears flooded my eyes and she held me while I sobbed. I finally felt free to express my grief. A bereaved sibling who attended Compassionate Friends stated, "This is the first time anyone has asked, 'What happened to you?' Finally, someone has acknowledged that my brother's death didn't just happen to my parents; it happened to me, too."

Take time to seek out the children in a bereaved family. If they don't want to talk, then just play a game, read a book, or watch a favorite TV program with them. Children often feel that if bad things happen to them it must mean they are bad. As a friend or family member, you can help preserve their feelings of self-worth by spending time with them, hugging them, and praising them for their accomplishments.

Continuing normal patterns as much as possible will help give a child a feeling of security. One friend whose father was killed on the mission field when she was seven remembers the birthday party her mother prepared for her just two days after her father's death as one of the nicest parties she ever had. I'm sure that party was difficult for her mother, but it helped the little girl feel there were still some traditions and some people she could depend on. As a teenager, she also remembers feeling sad as she watched other girls being kissed by their dads, but she is grateful for her two brothers who gave her lots of special attention and many hugs.

A boy whose father has died needs the attention of a man, someone who will take him to a ball game or sit in the stands and cheer for him while he plays on the school team, confirming that he is a person of value.

The program at a recent Compassionate Friends convention included a special panel for bereaved siblings. The most common complaint from the young people was how fearful and overprotective their parents had become since their brother's or sister's death. The parents' fear is understandable, but it is important to give the remaining children freedom to live normal lives. At least be open with them. "Since your brother died in a car accident, I'm nervous about letting you take the car. I'll do a lot better if you make every effort to be home on time and always call if you are delayed."

Several summers after Nate's accident a ten-year-old girl stayed with us for two weeks. One evening she went bike riding with some friends. While they were gone, we heard several sirens in our area. I got so nervous, I was almost in tears by the time the girls returned. I told her that those sirens reminded me of the sirens I heard the night Nate died, and silly as my reaction may seem, I would really feel better if she only went riding when Glen or I could go with her. Once she understood my feelings, she accepted my request quite willingly.

Getting over your fears and giving children room to enjoy life will take a while, but if you're honest with each other, your children will be more likely to cooperate with you. Teenagers may have a particularly difficult time dealing with the death of someone close. Because of their youth, their grief is often minimized by adults, yet teenagers are old enough to feel the pain very deeply and also to feel the pain of others. While grieving for Nathan, I discovered that when I shared my feelings with some of his teenage friends, they were able to empathize with me better than many adults. The young people at Nate's school weren't afraid to acknowledge their grief. They were the ones who thought of giving me the roses at graduation and presenting the slide show at baccalaureate. They dared to speak openly about their love for Nathan and how much they missed him.

I often received notes like these:

> I just wanted to take this time to tell you that I'm still thinking of you and praying for you. I hope my smile and questions about how you're doing make your days easier. Let me know if you need someone to talk to or do something for you.
>
> Mickey

> When I see you in the halls, I can see that you are having a very hard time. I want you to know that if there was anything in the whole world that I could do that would lessen your hurt, I would gladly do it. When I see you hurt, it just hurts me so much inside I can hardly stand it. I can now truly understand 1 Corinthians 12:26 [NIV] that talks about the body of Christ: "If one part suffers, every part suffers with it; if one part is honored, every part rejoices with it." We all hurt with you, Mrs. Heavilin!
>
> Natalie

On the first anniversary of Nate's death, I received this note from one of my former students:

> I just wanted you to know that I was think-
> ing about you today. I know this must be a
> difficult time for you. Nathan was very special
> to all of us, and even though I miss him
> greatly, I'm sure I can't begin to understand
> the depths of your love for him and the mixed
> emotions you must have at this time. I only
> pray that God will continue to comfort you
> with the awesome fact that Nathan beat the
> rest of us home!
>
> Andy

We need to be careful not to rebuff young people's attempts to express their sorrow. Sometimes we can help them by verbalizing feelings they might be having. "When an older brother dies, sometimes a younger brother can feel very lonely. He might even be mad at his brother because he left so suddenly. Do you ever feel like that?"

If our children don't seem comfortable sharing their feelings with us, we need to help them find someone they can talk to: school counselor, teacher, pastor, youth worker, grief counselor, or peer.

Reach out to bereaved children, spend time with them and find out how they're feeling. They are innocent, fragile rosebuds who need gentle, loving care. Be a rose and help them through this difficult, confusing time.

The Rose
of
Uniqueness

I will praise thee; for I am fearfully and wonderfully made: marvellous are thy works; and that my soul knoweth right well (Psalms 139:14).

When I first met Glen Heavilin, I knew I had met my perfect match. He was quiet, steady, and dependable. He thought through everything he did, and didn't speak until he had something important to say. He was all of the things I wasn't!

He listened quietly while I talked on and on and was content to let me get involved in lots of committees and social groups while he stayed home and studied or

watched the children. His mood was predictable—peaceful and happy—while mine constantly changed. He provided me with dependability and I provided him with
variety.

It really has been a good match. We've had very few
major arguments. I have disagreed with him often, but I
soon discovered it was no fun to argue with someone
who wouldn't argue back. So we began to do it Glen's
way: We reasoned with each other and settled things
peacefully. His way worked just fine until Nathan's
death.

We were grieving differently and our marriage was
being tested. It hadn't been that way with the deaths of
Jimmy and Ethan, and we knew we now had to find out
what the problems were. Before, our strength had been
in our love, our concern, and our admiration for each
other. After Nate's death those things didn't seem to be
enough. We were disagreeing on everything and we
couldn't understand why.

With the other boys' deaths, there was no one to blame,
no legal hassles. With Nate's death, waiting for all the
legal and insurance matters to be settled was like waiting
for the benediction at the funeral, and it slowed down the
healing process. Going to court again and again, only to
find the trial date had been postponed, was like a ham-
mer blow driving me lower and lower into the depths of
despair.

Our case was postponed eleven times and then actually
was settled on the one day we didn't go because the
district attorney felt the trial would just be postponed
again. We felt cheated. We did not have a chance to hear
the man declared guilty; nor did we have a chance to
speak regarding his sentencing—one more frustration in
the long line of bewildering legal proceedings.

An organization such as MADD could have given us
professional help, but there was no chapter in our area,

and we were too tired and confused to try to get help beyond our local area. I wish a counselor or a friend had been able to do that for us.

Having to deal with the manslaughter case was very discouraging because we felt so uninformed and excluded. No one ever volunteered any information; we had to dig to find out what was going on. When the case was finally resolved, the man was sentenced to three years of probation and not a day in jail.

If you are a pastor or counselor, or a friend of the bereaved person, please understand that that person needs to express his feelings in whatever way is comfortable for him without fear of condemnation. I was angry at a justice system that in my opinion didn't hand out a punishment equal to the crime, and I became quite cynical. Some of my feelings were not the best, yet I needed to express them. But when people responded with, "You're a Christian; you shouldn't feel like that," I was devastated.

I thought, *It's true that I'm a Christian, but I'm still having these feelings. Is there something wrong with me?* It was much more helpful when someone let me say how I felt and then worked with me to resolve those feelings without condemning me.

In regard to the insurance, we felt vulnerable because we had so little control. Our objective was to get the insurance settled as soon as possible. The amount of the settlement concerned us to a point—we felt it had to be adequate because to us it represented Nate's "worth" and we could not accept the possibility we might receive less because he was "not an only child" or because he was "only seventeen." On the other hand, it didn't have to be exorbitant; we had few bills to pay and we were not dependent on Nate for financial support.

The other families felt they needed to take plenty of time to make sure the doctors had discovered all of the injuries their children had incurred—the larger the settlement, the more they would have available to "protect their child's future." This was hard for us since Glen and I had discovered years ago that only God can protect our children's futures.

We realized their goals were different from ours, but Glen's reaction to that was opposite to mine. He felt we had no choice but to wait since our insurance company did not want to settle with us until they could settle with everyone. He even suggested we should wait patiently!

Well, I waited because I had no choice, but I certainly didn't wait patiently. I fussed and fumed. I wanted Glen to call the other families and demand that they understand what they were doing to us by dragging everything out so long. Glen wouldn't do that, and he didn't want me to do much either, so I spent my time being mad at Glen. Our marriage was full of stress. Many times it took several vigorous walks around the block together before we could even speak to each other.

We were both vulnerable and our weaknesses began to reveal themselves. My need to talk began to bother Glen. He didn't want to hear all about my difficult days because his days were difficult, too. My up-and-down moods turned into all down ones, and I cried frequently.

The insurance situation and the manslaughter trial together wore me down, and I didn't want to reason—I wanted to fight. Glen didn't look like a peacemaker to me anymore; he looked like Mr. Milquetoast. I wanted him to protect me from the cold, cruel world and make people be nice to me. Instead, he kept telling me I should be patient with the insurance company and with the court system. The more I nagged him to get involved, the more uninvolved he became.

That fall I attended a seminar led by Florence Littauer where she talked about temperaments and gave each person a temperament test. After I discovered what my temperament was, I went home and had Glen take the same test. Then I began to understand why we were having difficulty. Our temperaments were opposite, which is typical of most couples. Most of the time that's wonderful because your partner has strengths where you have weaknesses and you can build each other up.

If you're a serious person, it's nice to have someone who is fun, can tell jokes, and sees the funny side of life. But those same things that are fun and make you mesh together when everything is going right also tend to pull you apart when you're going through tragedy.

I believe that as married couples we often don't understand each other and so we do not recognize our partner's needs. Those needs are built into their temperaments.

There are four basic temperaments: Sanguine, Choleric, Melancholy, and Phlegmatic. Glen's major temperament is Phlegmatic: "low-key personality, easygoing and relaxed, calm, cool, and collected, happily reconciled to life, an all-purpose person."[1]

Some of the Phlegmatic's weaknesses are: "avoids responsibility, quiet will of iron, too compromising, resents being pushed, stays uninvolved, resists change."[2]

My temperament is a split of Choleric and Melancholy: "must correct wrongs, strong-willed and decisive, moves quickly to action, insists on production, idealistic, persistent and thorough, sees the problems."[3] Some of a Choleric/Melancholy's weaknesses are: "impatient, demanding of others, remembers the negatives, moody and depressed, self-centered, persecution complex, depressed over imperfections, hard to please, critical of others, dislikes those in opposition, unforgiving."[4]

No wonder we were having trouble! Our basic responses to adversity were so different. As I listened to Florence I began to realize that Glen was not responding differently from me just to buck me, and he wasn't necessarily saying I was wrong. We simply were looking at the world through different eyes.

Each temperament is driven by different goals. The Sanguine wants to have fun; the Choleric wants to have control; the Melancholy wants to have it right; and the Phlegmatic wants to have peace.

So Glen's goal was to have peace: "Don't rock the boat"; my goal was to have control and have everything right. When Nathan died, all of our goals were challenged.

Glen recalls:

Marilyn mentioned the manslaughter trial, which is a criminal operation run by the district attorney's office. In some countries of the world the victim has a voice in criminal cases, but the victim has no voice in our criminal justice system.

Marilyn is Choleric/Melancholy. The Melancholy wants everything to be perfect and the Choleric wants to control things to make them just and fair and equitable.

Now how do you control the criminal justice system? The Phlegmatic says, "Anybody in his right mind knows you cannot control the criminal justice system."

Marilyn would say, "Why don't you call the district attorney and find out what's happening with the case?" My brain says, "Why would I want to do that? We'll find out what's happening with the case when the district attorney does something with it. . . ." I learned how to call the district attorney. Marilyn learned how to, as gently as possible, prod me into calling. She really did. You have to gently prod a Phlegmatic. If you sternly prod a

Phlegmatic, he sets his heels in and says, "I will not do it," and I've done that many times.

It is important to take the time to recognize that others are different, and to give them the space to be different. Be creative and look for ways you can meet the other person's needs. It will pay off.

While I am talking basically about the husband and wife relationship, you can adopt these principles with your children and your friends as well. Our daughter Mellyn has a temperament much like her father's. She did not want me to cry; she wanted things to stay as normal as possible. She didn't need a lot of people around and often retreated to her apartment when our house became crowded with people. I needed lots of people around and became depressed when everyone left.

Since Mellyn didn't want me to cry, I made sure I didn't cry in front of her. One day when Mellyn was in our home, I was very depressed. Because I felt I couldn't cry in front of her, I went into my bedroom, called my friend Nancy, and told her I needed help. Nancy quickly came to the house and told Mellyn I had called her. When Mellyn came to the bedroom and found me sobbing, she was very hurt because I hadn't told her I was having a hard time.

We finally realized neither one of us was wrong but we were grieving differently, and we needed to make room for each other.

I began to understand that Mellyn missed Nate terribly even though she didn't show it in the same ways I did. Mellyn learned that each time I cried, I healed just a little bit more.

Our son Nathan was a strong Phlegmatic just like his father. I had learned to adjust to Glen, but when one of my children was so different from me, I had difficulty. As a Choleric mother I insisted each child make his or her bed every day, but Nate couldn't see any need in making his bed because after all, "I'll just get back into it tonight." I'm the type who wants to have everything done two weeks ahead of time, but Nate would say, "Why hurry to read the book? I have two days before I have to turn my book report in."

I wish now I had understood the temperaments when I was rearing my children. I've had to go to my remaining children and say, "I need to apologize to you for some of the ways I worked with you because I just didn't understand."

Understanding our temperaments has helped us to realize what our normal first reaction would be in a given situation. Now we are able to work on our deficiencies and emphasize our strengths without feeling the other person is disapproving of our behavior.

The Sanguine's basic underlying drive is to have *fun*. If he loses his fun, he gets depressed. The Sanguine child can't sit very long in class, and he will have difficulty listening to a lecture unless the speaker is entertaining. Sanguines want to get involved, and when they enter a crowd, they see an audience to entertain. They have a childlike style of emotion even when they reach adulthood. Their emotions can be very short-lived and changeable. They cry hard but a few minutes later they can go on to something else.

Sanguines will come bouncing into a room and never know a stranger. They make wonderful waitresses, receptionists, salespeople, comedians, and talk show hosts. They talk very easily to everyone. If others don't talk, they just keep on talking and don't even notice because they like to hear themselves talk. When they're angry, their anger generally doesn't last long. Once they have said everything they want to say, it's over and everything is fine. They can't understand what's wrong with all of those other people who are mad at them. When a Sanguine is grieving, he will try to forget his troubles by having fun.

Sanguines need constant encouragement and approval. You can keep a Sanguine going as long as you keep telling him he's doing a good job and keep recognizing his efforts.

The Choleric's major drive is for *control*. When Cholerics go through trauma, they try to deny the pain by becoming totally absorbed in their work, a hobby, or a social cause. They'll work furiously and may not want to come home for fear it will be too emotional and they might lose control.

The one emotion Cholerics may display is anger, and their anger is generally rooted in impatience because things aren't moving, people are slow, and they don't see any progress. They also may display anger when they're actually feeling sadness.[5] It is almost impossible for Cholerics to say "I'm sorry," even if they feel it inside because admitting blame makes them feel they're losing control or becoming vulnerable to other people.

Cholerics have a need for appreciation of responsible and dutiful endeavors. They need acknowledgment of their hard work. Some men come home after putting in many extra hours at work to hear their wives say, "I don't feel you love me anymore. I never see you. You don't seem concerned. You aren't involved with us."

The husband responds, "But I work sixty hours a week for you. What more do you want?" From the Choleric's point of view, he is showing love by the amount of work he produces, but it may not mean a thing to the wife who is home alone and needs to have some attention from her husband. It helps if we can understand how each temperament directs our method of demonstrating love and concern for others.

Melancholies want *perfection*. They want to be able to depend on how things are going to be; they're generally quite methodical. They will have medium highs but they have very low lows. A melancholy trying to deal with grief may go into a deep depression.

When Melancholies are depressed, everybody knows it. Some of them get to the point where they don't talk at all. I didn't get that low, but I did have occasions when I felt a cloud of doom was over my head and I couldn't get away from it. At those times, having people around me who wanted to have fun was totally obnoxious to me. I couldn't understand the responses of those people because I felt deeply about everything.

In *Personality Patterns*, Lana Bateman refers to the Melancholies as "green stamp collectors." When you hurt them they take a green stamp and paste it into their book. If somebody else hurts them, they paste down another green stamp. They may be holding their feelings inside but they have all of these green stamps in the book. When that last green stamp gets in the book, it may be something very simple, it may not be nearly as big a hurt as something on the first page of their green-stamp book, but they may explode.[6]

One day after we moved into our new home, we couldn't find something (I can't even remember what it was), but after I looked and looked and couldn't find it, I just fell apart. I sobbed and sobbed. It had very little to do with what I couldn't find, but my emotions had built up through our move and the dam finally broke. Poor Glen was standing there trying to think what he had done wrong.

The Melancholy's underlying need is "Creative Tenderness."[7] Melancholies are very good about thinking of ways to show creative tenderness but they tend to marry temperaments that don't really notice all of their effort. The Melancholy thinks up wonderful ideas and wishes someone would do those things for him. I've had to learn to communicate my needs and desires to others. Phlegmatics have a great desire for *peace*, sometimes peace at any price. They fear conflict, and it is very hard for them to express their emotions. Phlegmatics may show little emotion even when they are experiencing grief, and those around them may think they have already worked through their grief. In truth, it could be they have not handled it at all. It may take them several years before they deal with their loss. They often respond to anger with sadness which is just the opposite of the Choleric who usually responds to sadness with anger. When these two temperaments marry each other, and that will frequently happen because opposites tend to marry, they are likely to have problems.

As a Choleric, when I'm sad about something, my sadness may come out in anger as it did when I was faced with the insurance problems. I wanted Glen to go tell the other families what this was doing to us. Why couldn't they understand? I was angry because I was hurt. Glen pulled back and wanted to be really quiet about it. He wanted to keep peace.

I said to Glen, "You aren't protecting me. You aren't taking care of me and meeting my needs. What's wrong with you? I don't know you anymore." And I'm sure Glen felt the same about me.

Phlegmatics need a sense of value—they need to feel they're important. Because they have difficulty showing emotion or expressing their thoughts, they are often lost in the crowd and it's easy for people to assume they have no thoughts. The partner who sticks with them, though, will eventually find out what's going on in the Phlegmatic's mind.

Understanding the temperaments will help when you and your family are in a crisis. The death of a child may be the worst thing you have ever faced in your life, and differences in temperaments can increase the stress within the entire family. You need to remember that other family members loved that child as much as you did. Don't alienate them. Reach out to them. Pull them in so you can enjoy together the love and memories you shared and try to learn the underlying needs of each other. Recovering from grief can be a life-changing experience. (One book I recommend to help you better understand the different temperaments is *Personality Plus* by Florence Littauer.)

It is important that we give other family members room to grieve in their own way, but we also need to work at keeping in touch with each other. Some of the things Glen and I did were to talk and listen to each other. I brought the temperament test home and I said, "I know you don't like this kind of thing, but I need you to listen." As I read the characteristics of the Phlegmatic, I described Glen right down the line.

Glen said, "Let me see that." Sure enough, this test had him pegged. I asked, "What do you want me to do for you? How can I help you?"

He said, "I need peace and quiet." It was easy to spot our difficulty when I said, "I need to talk. I need to tell someone how I feel, why I get mad, upset, and frustrated every time this trial gets postponed. Yet I realize that when I talk to you it upsets you, and you feel helpless. I know you can't do anything about the justice system, but I still need to get it out."

Finally Glen said, "Well, when you get upset, why don't you call Joan or go see Nancy?" This was a concession for Glen because we always had the policy that we didn't talk about our personal problems outside of our family. He realized, though, that in this situation he was helpless. He couldn't do anything about it, and when he heard me complain he just got more depressed and felt more inadequate. He said, "You need to have someone you can talk to who won't feel the load like I feel it."

Once I aired my feelings with someone else, I could

come home and love Glen. We began to understand it was all right to be different. Just because I was doing something one way didn't mean the way Glen was doing it was wrong.

As we were listing our needs and desires, Glen said, "I need to know that you aren't disappointed in me, that you aren't angry with me or blaming me because this insurance situation isn't going better." I hadn't realized that when I let off steam about our situation I was pushing Glen deeper into a hole of guilt. I just knew I needed confirmation that he thought I was doing all right and that he still liked me.

We planned special times to be together. We drove to the mountains, walked around Lake Arrowhead, and talked. Sometimes we just drove to a nearby regional park, ate dinner in our motorhome, and talked. Where we were didn't matter, but talking did. We became reacquainted and slowly began to rediscover those special traits that had drawn us together originally.

I can now say after thirty-five years of marriage that we really are enjoying those differences again. Glen's sense of humor, for a while an irritant to me, is now wonderful—nice and dry. I appreciate his ability to be a peacemaker although right after Nate's death I didn't want peace. Glen does not enjoy traveling and speaking as much as I do, but he has given me room to do so because I love it. He is my support system, and even travels with me when he can.

People often ask me, "What does poor Glen do while you are traveling?"

Without even a twinge of guilt, I can now say, "He enjoys some peace and quiet!" We back each other up now, but it has taken a great deal of effort and commitment to each other, our marriage, and to God to get to this point. Be assured, it has been worth every bit of effort!

Each of us can be a rose to the people in our families who are grieving differently from the way we are. Reach out to them and say, "It's okay that we're different, but the most important thing is that we stick together. We need each other. We loved this person together. We need to share our hurt together." You can be a rose of uniqueness if you make room for those you love.

How thrilling to realize that our precious Lord created each of us to grow in His garden as unique, priceless roses.

The Rose
of
Tenderness

O Lord, don't hold back your tender mercies from me! My only hope is in your love and faithfulness. Otherwise I perish, for problems far too big for me to solve are piled higher than my head (Psalms 40:11-12 TLB).

After Nate's death, many people said to Glen and me, "You'll find this crisis will draw you closer together." Now, after several years of working through our differences, I believe we are closer, but that wasn't true at first. For many couples crisis pulls their families apart because crisis will accentuate nearly every aspect of your marriage, weak or strong. A salesman named Joe was trying to sell us a motor home, and in a talkative and friendly manner he asked about our family. We explained that we had two married children and then told him about Nate.

He started asking some very knowledgeable questions. "How have you dealt with the grief? Your marriage seems to be okay. How have you managed that?"

I said, "Joe, what's your story? I sense you have dealt with a major loss."

His eyes filled with tears as he recalled, "My second wife and I had been married just a few months. My son came to visit one weekend. He was riding his bike near our house when he was struck and killed by a drunk driver.

"He was my only son. When he died, everything in my life changed. For the next year I spent all of my time following the manslaughter trial. Nothing else mattered. The driver was given a light sentence which didn't satisfy me, and I was consumed with anger.

"My new wife didn't know my son well, and she couldn't relate to my grief. Soon, we stopped talking to each other. I stayed away from home as much as I could. I blamed myself—why did I let him ride on that busy street? I should have gone with him.

"I became more and more depressed. Our marriage ended within a year."

Joe looked wistfully at Glen and me and said, "If you can survive the deaths of three sons, you've got something pretty special."

Joe was right. Any couple whose marriage weathers a crisis as severe as the death of a child is in the minority today. Compassionate Friends states that between 75 and 85 percent of the couples who lose a child will divorce within the first five years after the death. Will you be one of the statistics? You don't have to be if you're willing to work at keeping your marriage together. Let's look at some factors which tend to break up a marriage.

Guilt. It is natural for a person to experience guilt, deserved or undeserved, when a loved one dies, but it is destructive when the guilt is allowed to fester and grow out of proportion. We need to talk to someone openly about our feelings.

When Nate died, one of my first thoughts was, Why didn't I go to the game with him? This wouldn't have happened if I had been there.

By the time I told Glen how I felt, I had built a strong case against myself. In an effort to help me analyze my feelings, Glen said, "Why didn't you go to the game?"

"Well, I had been to one on Tuesday and I was going to the game on Friday. Also, I would have had to drive to Hemet alone, fifty miles away, at night, and I've never done that before."

Glen very logically said, "So even if you had gone, you probably would not have been in the same car with Nate."

"Well, probably not," I admitted.

Glen continued, "If you had been in the car with Nate, how could you have prevented the crash?"

"I don't know, but mothers are supposed to be able to protect their children!" I sobbed.

In a very loving and yet logical way, Glen helped me see how unwarranted my guilt was.

Blame. Although it may not be justified, couples often build a case of blame against each other. A husband may think, *If she hadn't let him play in the front yard, he wouldn't have been able to run out into the street,* even though they had both allowed the child to play in the front yard on previous occasions. Whether or not the husband is justified in blaming his wife, these feelings must be carefully and sensitively exposed, discussed, and eliminated, or a wedge will start to form between them.

Lack of communication. Often a wife will tell me, "He never talks anymore. I don't know what he's thinking. He eats and sleeps at our house, but that's it. We're strangers." A spouse's grief may be so all-consuming that he can't risk talking about it for fear of losing control. Getting this person to open up will take a lot of tender, patient probing.

Not understanding sexual needs. When Laura and Jim's daughter died, they were both overwhelmed with grief, but they responded differently. Within a few days after their daughter's death, Jim wanted to have sexual relations with Laura; he needed that emotional release and the assurance that she still cared for him.

Laura was indignant. "How can you think about enjoying yourself like that when we just buried our daughter?"

Couples who have lost little children may have opposing responses also. I heard one young father say, "I think we should have another baby right away." His wife responded, "I'm afraid of getting pregnant. I don't ever want to love anyone that much again."

These are all normal responses but they can cause difficulty if they are not discussed and resolved. A wife who is afraid of being sexually intimate will still usually enjoy being held and tenderly cared for. Be sensitive to each other's needs, concerns, and fears. Give each other time.

Expecting too much of ourselves. I am quite melancholic in my temperament and am very much the martyr, so it takes me a long time to admit I've had enough. One evening in May, after Nate had died in February, I reached a point of total desperation. I sobbed, "I can't ever go back to school. I have to get out of here."

Glen could have just given me a pep talk saying something like, "You're a big girl now. You need to get hold of yourself and get on with life." Instead he chose to show me the tenderness I needed, and very calmly said, "Where do you want to go?"

I really didn't care, but the first place that popped into my mind was Hawaii. That was a Thursday evening; we left on Sunday! I'm sure the travel agent wondered about us. She asked, "Which islands do you wish to visit?"

Glen and I shrugged our shoulders and he said, "We don't care. You decide."

Then she queried, "What hotel would you like to stay at?"

Again the answer came, "We don't care. You decide."

We really didn't care. We knew we had to get away, but the place or the hotel simply didn't matter. Nothing mattered right then except that our son was dead and we were hurting.

With mixed emotions, I said goodbye to my remaining two children on Mother's Day morning. I felt a twinge of guilt because I was leaving them, but I knew we had to do this. Was I running away? Perhaps, but I decided it was all right. Even Jesus had to get away from the crowds once in a while.

I wrote in my journal:

Today is the day we fly to Hawaii! I still can hardly believe it, but I am getting excited. That excitement is mixed with twinges of remorse and guilt. Remorse because of why we need this trip, and guilt because we're trying to enjoy ourselves so soon after Nate's death and because I've never been away from my kids on Mother's Day. I felt funny leaving them.

Today I have been able to handle the verse about "forgetting the things that are behind." I believe I am beginning to desire that, but until now, that verse just made me angry. I have been fighting against that verse, so I

know this desire to "forge ahead" has to be
from the Lord. It surely didn't come from me.
Perhaps a new day is dawning—one in which
we can build a future with new memories and
let the old memories rest. I hope so.

The next day: "I awoke this morning with the same old
thought, Nate is gone. But it didn't hit me like a kick in
the stomach; it was more like a 'nagging backache.' It's
always there, but I'm learning to live with it."

The trip to Hawaii was good for us; it was our first
extended vacation without the children in twenty-four
years. The trip helped us begin to build some memories
which didn't include Nate and it gave us a temporary
release from the pressures at home.

Since that time, Glen and I have traveled to Japan,
England, and Australia, and made a return trip to Hawaii. Those trips took effort on our part. Most of the time
it would have been easier to stay home and wallow in our
misery. I didn't enjoy tending to all of the details traveling requires, and it was hard to move out into a new
environment, but it did help. Now we don't wait for the
pressure to build up so high. We take small trips often,
and our marriage has become stronger because we have
spent time alone with each other away from all of the
reminders and problems.

Lack of special attention. In the face of the personal and
family tragedy that we were dealing with, I needed a way
to communicate to Glen that he was important to me.
Nathan was important and his death was important, but
Glen needed to feel that in spite of all that was happening
around him, he was important, too.

After some of the dust had settled, I said, "Glen, I want
you to choose a day and take off work. In fact it would
be even better if you took a day and a half."

"Why?"

"I'll tell you later."

When the day came, I gave Glen a list of instructions. "Get in the car. Drive down Cajon Avenue. Turn left at the next traffic signal. . . ." We followed this little sequence of clues and ended up at a Victorian mansion which was a bed-and-breakfast inn. In the trunk of our car nestled a wicker picnic basket with a chilled bottle of sparkling cider, cookies, cheese, fresh fruit, and a tape recorder with a cassette of "Music for Lovers." We spent the evening in this Victorian mansion with a player grand piano which Glen loved, and I had the opportunity to show Glen some tenderness and say, "In spite of all we're going through, you're important to me. You are a very important person."

Personal responses to grief. Glen and I led a workshop on "How We All Grieve Differently" for the National Convention of The Compassionate Friends in Omaha, Nebraska. When we finished, Nancy, one of the conferees, stood and gave a beautiful example of how she found a way to meet her husband's needs even though they were grieving differently and he seemed unable to express his feelings to her.

> Before our son was killed my husband and I always had a good marriage. Even though we've had lots of tragedy, we always managed to get through everything. But after our son died, my husband just clammed up. He didn't want to have anything to do with me; he didn't talk. He just went to work, went to the cemetery, came home, and that was it. This went on for two years.
>
> I felt completely abandoned. I had six other kids and they looked to me for emotional help, but when it came to me, I was on my own. This was the worst time to be on my own. I didn't

understand him. I began to resent the fact that my husband wasn't there for me as he had always been when we went through so many other things.

Finally, I don't know why I thought of it, but I got a notebook and I started to write to him in the notebook. I left it in his underwear drawer where he would have to see it. I wrote about all sorts of things, things I was feeling, things I knew he was feeling. I wrote about how good he was all through our marriage when different things happened and told him what a great guy he was. I told him I didn't know what had happened, but I felt I didn't have him anymore.

He always read my notes, but he never said a word. After a whole year of me writing in the notebook and sticking it in his drawer, he finally came out of his shell. It was almost three years after our son's death, and now our marriage is better than it has ever been. Having a good relationship with him again is worth all of the effort I put forth.

Even though they were grieving differently, and her husband had isolated himself, Nancy found a way to extend loving tenderness to him.

In an article on coping with heartbreak, Robert Veninga states: "When a husband and wife share a heartbreak, each must plot his or her own defense. You cannot plan the defense strategies of your partner nor can you plot a joint defense, for a heartbreak really is a solitary experience."[1]

In many ways grief is a solitary experience, but you can be a rose of tenderness as you make the effort to tell your spouse how you feel and what your needs are. We are extremely fragile people at this point, but we will become stronger as we can spread the fragrance of our roses around us and we realize what is important to us. Don't let go of those loved ones you have. Don't let the differences part you. Bring yourselves together. Keep looking for the roses. They're there.

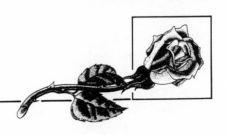

The Rose of Love

But God showed his great love for us by sending Christ to die for us while we were still sinners (Romans 5:8 TLB).

Without the Rose of Love there would be no book because I would have no hope. The Rose of Love is my best Friend, my Comforter, and my Redeemer. He is revealed in the Bible as God, Jesus Christ, and the Holy Spirit. Through the years, as I have learned more about God and as He has let me see how much He loves and cares for me, He has become my best Friend. He never criticizes me; He always listens when I need to talk; and He is constantly looking out for my best interests.

As I have experienced the deaths of three of my sons,

God has become my Comforter. He is always available to me; He is not impatient with me; He doesn't judge me or rebuke me for admitting I hurt. God has experienced sorrow. He, in fact, was a bereaved parent, because He, too, had a Son who suffered and died. But the exciting news is God's Son didn't stay dead. He conquered death for each of us so that we can have the hope of spending eternity with Him in heaven. We also can have the hope of seeing our loved ones again.

I have vivid memories of a special night when Nate was five years old. I was tucking him into bed and he seemed restless and unable to settle down. I asked him if there was a problem. He squirmed a little and then said, "I'm not sure I've invited Jesus into my heart."

I asked him why he wanted to invite Jesus into his life. "Because I've done some wrong things, and I want to make sure I'll go to heaven."

I listened as Nathan prayed and asked Jesus to come into his heart and live with him. After that there was no doubt in Nate's mind. He referred to the event often. As he grew, we saw the effect of the decision in his desire to study God's Word and in his submissive attitude toward us and toward God. How thankful I am I can look back on that evening and have confidence I will see Nate again.

"And now, dear brothers, I want you to know what happens to a Christian when he dies so that when it happens, you will not be full of sorrow, as those are who have no hope. For since we believe that Jesus died and then came back to life again, we can also believe that when Jesus returns, God will bring back with him all the Christians who have died" (1 Thess. 4:13-14 TLB). Jesus understands my sorrow. He experienced abuse, rejection, and death. He wept when others were grieving. He felt their sorrow and He feels my sorrow and yours. Jesus comforts us so we can comfort others. He wants us to pass it on. God, in the person of the Holy Spirit, comforts my heart, assures me I will see my children again, and gives me the power to live my life as a victor rather than a victim.

It is my prayer that this little book will be helpful to all who read it whether they know Jesus as their personal Savior or not. However, it is important for you to understand the reason I have been able to accept Jimmy's, Ethan's, and Nathan's deaths. It is primarily because of the source of strength available to me through Jesus Christ, the Rose of Love.

If you do not know Jesus, I encourage you to invite Him into your life now. Jesus has extended the invitation to you: "Come unto me, all ye that labour and are heavy laden, and I will give you rest" (Matt. 11:28).

Some of you may not want to deal with this right now. Perhaps you have "put God on hold." You may be asking a lot of questions: How could a God of love let my child suffer and die? or Why my child? I talked with one bereaved parent who recalled, "At first I asked why, and then the question came back, Why not? Who am I to say my family should be exempt from trouble? Am I really more deserving of a trouble-free life than my neighbor or my friend?"

I cannot solve all of life's complex problems, and I, like you, certainly have asked why and haven't come up with profound answers. But I do know God loved each of us enough to offer His only Son as the perfect and permanent sacrifice so that you and I might have eternal life.

The same God who loved Glen and me enough to provide a sacrifice for our sins also allowed some people we loved dearly to die sooner than we thought they should. I can't explain God or God's ways, but I am confident enough of His love for me, and for Jimmy, Ethan, and Nathan, to say, "I trust Him and you can trust Him, too."

If you are experiencing grief, I'm sure you have many questions. You probably feel heavy laden, and you undoubtedly wish you could cast your burdens on someone else so that you could rest. I urge you right now to talk with Jesus and tell Him this is the heaviest burden you have ever had to bear. You are grieving because of a great loss and you are so very tired. Hand Him your burden and ask Him to carry it for you.

Jesus is the most beautiful Rose of all. Take a deep breath of the fragrance of His love and compassion and then perhaps you can share His fragrance by reaching out to others who are hurting, too.

Let the Rose of Love stand in the center of your bouquet of December roses.

The Rose
of
Confidence

In quietness and in confidence shall be your strength (Isaiah 30:15).

As I travel around the country and talk with the bereaved, I learn more and more that when someone dies, often the most non-religious people begin to think about God and even the most religious begin to ask questions about God.

I have been a Christian for more than fifty years. I have read through the Bible many times, and I have had the privilege of sitting under the teaching of some noted Bible teachers. Yet each time one of my sons died I struggled with who God is and what influence He has in the day-to-day happenings of my life. I want to share with you what I have discovered through personal Bible study, questioning of Bible scholars, and personal observation. I want you to know that it's okay to examine the reasons for the events in our lives.

When our twin sons were born on Christmas morning of 1965, just a year and a half after the death of our seven-week-old son Jimmy, we knew the twins were a special gift from the Lord. We wanted to tell the world how good God had been to us—giving us an extra son perhaps to pay us back for the one who had died. We sent out over a hundred birth announcements proclaiming Psalm 118:23: "This is the LORD'S doing; it is marvellous in our eyes."

It was easy to give God the credit when everything was going our way, but when Ethan died ten days later, I felt like God had tricked me. What would my friends think now? What could I say to them? God and I had many conversations in which I told Him how I felt, but as time went on, I began to see that God was using our experience to make us stronger and wiser people. He had also given us a special compassion for others, especially young boys. As my love began to grow for boys who were not my own but needed a second mother, I thought perhaps I could begin to see God's plan.

Then Nate died and I started to ponder things all over again: *This may be the Lord's doing, but it doesn't seem very marvelous in my eyes.* Why would God allow all of these things to happen to one family? Through the years I have discovered that the concept that bad things don't happen to good people is a myth, but I have still struggled with the question, Why do bad things happen to good people?

The first question I had to settle in my mind was, Does God really have anything to do with what happens to His children? Some people say, "Well, obviously He knows these things are going to happen because He is God and He knows everything, but He didn't plan them or allow them. A loving God wouldn't do that. He just watched while they happened."

Others say, "Satan is in control of this world at the present time, and God doesn't have anything to do with the bad things that happen to us. The consequences of sin are out of His control."

Then others say, "All of the bad things that happen to us are our fault because we have made wrong choices. We bring all of our problems on ourselves. They have nothing to do with God."

I listened to all of these comments, and I did not feel at peace with any of them. I couldn't see that my children or I had made wrong choices which could have caused their deaths. What wrong choice did Nate make? He was following all of the rules of the road, he wasn't playing around, he was obedient to his parents, he honored the Lord, but he is still dead. Jimmy and Ethan were too little to make choices, good or bad.

The Bible refers to Satan as the ruler of "the darkness of this world" (Eph. 6:12) and as "the god of this evil world" (2 Cor. 4:4 TLB), but it also teaches that even Satan is subject to God and cannot touch one of His children without God's knowledge and permission. "And the Lord replied to Satan, 'You may do anything you like with his wealth, but don't harm him physically' " (Job 1:12 TLB). " 'Do with him as you please,' the Lord replied; 'only spare his life' " (Job 2:6 TLB).

Although Satan is running free in this world, I always thought God had ultimate control over His children, those who had received Him as their personal Savior. Before Satan could touch God's servant Job, Satan asked God's permission.

I also reasoned that, since God is all-knowing and was aware that each of my children was dying, as He also is an all-powerful God, He had the capacity to change their situations if He so chose. He could have directed Nate to take a different road, kept the drunk driver off that road for a few seconds more, or simply allowed Nate to escape serious injury. I cannot conceive of serving a God who is powerful enough to rise from the dead but not powerful enough to control Satan. It seems to me that would make Satan more powerful than God, and if that's true, we're all in trouble!

As I read Scripture and reasoned through all of these theories, I came back to my previous conclusion: God allows His children to suffer. Then I began to search for an answer to the question, Why would a loving God allow His children to bear so much pain and suffering?

In a little booklet entitled *The Furnace of Affliction,* Pastor John Emmans presents three reasons God allows Christians to suffer: to comfort, to correct, and to conform.[1]

To comfort

The Bible teaches that God allows us to suffer so that we might be benefactors of His comfort and then be able to comfort others in His name.

> Blessed be God, even the Father of our Lord Jesus Christ, the Father of mercies, and the God of all comfort; Who comforteth us in all our tribulation, that we may be able to comfort them which are in any trouble, by the comfort wherewith we ourselves are comforted of God.   (2 Cor. 1:3-4)

Before Jimmy died, if a friend's child died, I would have sent a card and probably attended the funeral. The first time I saw them I might have acknowledged their loss, but I doubt that I would have mentioned the death again unless they brought it up. I would never have thought to remember them on the anniversary of the death or on the child's birthday. I think I would have been quite insensitive to their pain. When Jimmy died, as I was greeting friends at the funeral home, I noticed that those who had experienced a loss similar to mine were much more sensitive and concerned. They knew the hurt I felt and they understood how long that pain would last. They never said, "You should be over this by now." They knew how to comfort me.

Now, twenty-nine years and two more funerals later, I understand the special gift of comfort God gives to those He has allowed to suffer. As I sat with a radio host on a call-in talk show, we received many calls from grieving people. They would ask me questions and tell me their stories and the host would shake his head in disbelief. Sometimes he would look at me and helplessly shrug his shoulders as if to say, "What can you possibly say to help this person?"

As I listened, I silently prayed, "Lord, give me discernment to know what is really bothering this person. Let me sense where she has become stuck in the grieving process."

One lady whose Christian son had been involved in a fatal accident after drinking at a party told me she didn't feel comfortable at church anymore, but she didn't know why. As we talked she admitted she resented the people at church because her child had died and it didn't seem anyone else was having any trouble.

Then I said, "Mary, if I were in your situation, I think I would feel some anger toward my son."

I could hear the sobs on the other end of the line as Mary said, "I am so mad at him. He knew better. He knew how we felt about drinking. He embarrassed our family. Now I feel everyone at church is looking down on us. But then I think, 'He's dead. How dare you feel anger toward him.' And I go on a guilt trip and get depressed."

Later the radio host said, "How in the world did you know to ask Mary about her anger toward her son? I would never have thought of that."

I smiled and answered, "I've been there."

I've since communicated with Mary and she is working through her grief in a healthy way now that she has been able to identify where she was stuck. I know God uses my successes and my failures to help me help others in their grief work.

I recently received this letter:

> This past July I met and spoke for some time with you and your husband at the Christian Booksellers' Convention in Anaheim, California. I know you'll remember me, for we discussed our experiences with grief—the loss of your sons and for me, the loss of my husband. At that time you autographed your book for me and shared Romans 8:37: "But despite all this, overwhelming victory is ours through Christ who loved us enough to die for us" (TLB).
>
> Your book was truly a blessing to me. I read it when I got back home and since then I do "keep looking for the roses." The Lord's leading in my life since that day I spoke with you has been a special rose from the hand of God, for it has been the turning point that I've been searching for since my husband's death.
>
> The first two and a half years of widowhood found me looking for someone the Lord might have for me. Though I was willing to leave the choice with Him, it became increasingly difficult to accept that He had chosen not to send

that someone. Now because of having met you, reading your book and a number of other books, I feel the Lord leading me into a ministry for hurting people.

Since that day in California, He has taught me to stop dwelling so much on the past and move on with life. Thank you for caring and sharing with me, for being there at the right place and right time—His time—and for all you've meant to me.

I would never have chosen for my life to go in the direction it has, but when I read a letter like the one above, I feel grateful that I was in the right place at the right time. What a privilege to be able to comfort fellow sufferers, to encourage other weary souls and see them go on to serve the Lord and use their difficult experiences to comfort others.

To correct

You have forgotten that word of encouragement that addresses you as sons: "My son, do not make light of the Lord's discipline, and do not lose heart when he rebukes you, because the Lord disciplines those he loves, and he punishes everyone he accepts as a son."

Endure hardship as discipline; God is treating you as sons. For what son is not disciplined by his father? If you are not disciplined (and everyone undergoes discipline), then you are illegitimate children and not true sons. Moreover, we have all had human fathers who disciplined us and we respected them for it. How much more should we submit to the Father of our spirits and live! Our

> fathers disciplined us for a little while as they
> thought best; but God disciplines us for our
> good, that we may share in his holiness.
>
> No discipline seems pleasant at the time, but
> painful. Later on, however, it produces a har-
> vest of righteousness and peace for those who
> have been trained by it. (Heb. 12:5-11 NIV)

When troubles come our way, we would not be wise if
we didn't take time to examine ourselves and make sure
there are no obvious sins in our lives. Parents help children stay on the straight and narrow by disciplining them
when they stray from the right path, and the Bible teaches
that God will do the same thing when His children are
getting into trouble. Please understand, God's discipline
is not meted out as a vengeful punishment, a "getting
even." Rather, this word has more the connotation of
training and instruction. God, as our heavenly Father,
disciplines His children to teach them acceptable patterns of life and behavior, the same as responsible earthly
parents do.

When Nate died I did some soul-searching. Some people would say, "Certainly God wouldn't let your child
die because you were sinning," but Scripture would not
back up that theory. In fact when David sinned by getting involved with Bathsheba, the child born of that
union died.

"And David said unto Nathan, I have sinned against
the LORD. And Nathan said unto David, The LORD also
hath put away thy sin; thou shalt not die. Howbeit,
because by this deed thou hast given great occasion to the
enemies of the LORD to blaspheme, the child also that is
born unto thee shall surely die" (2 Sam. 12:13-14).

The Bible teaches that God does use suffering to discipline His children, but it does not support the theory

that all sickness, death, and suffering come because we are sinning.

To conform

I believe God has a special plan in mind when He allows suffering to come into our lives. However, I must admit that when I was in the midst of grief, I didn't really appreciate "friends" quoting "And we know that all things work together for good to them that love God, to them who are the called according to his purpose" (Rom. 8:28). I could see no good in the death of an innocent child.

Yet, as I read the verse which comes after that verse, Romans 8:28 became a little more palatable: "For whom he did foreknow, he also did predestinate to be conformed to the image of his Son, that he might be the firstborn among many brethren" (Rom. 8:29). So part of the good that is to come out of our troubles is that we conform to the image of Christ—we become more Christlike. The catch is, we have a choice—to be or not to be conformed.

Some years ago I attended a seminar conducted by Bill Gothard. He compared each Christian to a diamond in the rough. The diamond's beauty will be revealed through the polishing process. Our lives are like diamonds, and how much diamond is left after the polishing process of life depends on how much we resist the bumps and bruises along the way. The diamonds cannot be polished without friction, nor man perfected without trial.

When you're in trouble, what kind of a person would you turn to for help—one who has never had any troubles and has seemed to float through life on the proverbial "cloud nine"? I don't think so. I think we tend to be drawn toward a person who has been through a polishing process, one who has become strong through adversity. I want to be one of those strong people, a diamond that has not resisted the polishing process.

We have a choice to make. We can become defiant and say, "I will never serve a God who allows such terrible things to happen," or we can be confident that even though we don't understand why God has allowed these events to come into our lives, "He that keepeth thee will not slumber" (Ps. 121:3).

He has a plan for each of us individually. "The steps of a good man are ordered by the LORD: and he delighteth in his way. Though he fall, he shall not be utterly cast down: for the LORD upholdeth him with his hand" (Ps. 37:23-24).

The Rose of Surrender

But despite all this, overwhelming victory is ours through Christ who loved us enough to die for us (Romans 8:37 TLB).

I agree with the three reasons we discussed in the previous chapter that Pastor Emmans gave as to why God allows suffering. It is true that God allows His children to learn how to comfort others by receiving comfort from God; He uses difficult times to discipline His children; and He uses the hard times in our lives to conform us to His image.

I agree with these three reasons, but I would like to add a few more observations. I believe God allows troubles and trials to come into the lives of His children to reveal to us our insufficiency, His sufficiency, and His sovereignty.

I have never been more aware of my insufficiency, my inability to control the happenings in my own life, as when I stood near my child while his life slipped away. I realized my only hope was in the Lord. As King David pleaded for his child's life, he, too, recognized his insufficiency to change the course of events, but through his experiences he adopted the philosophy which he presents in Psalm 34:19: "The good man does not escape all troubles—he has them too. But the Lord helps him in each and every one" (TLB).

David made the choice to acknowledge his own inability to escape trouble and follow the God who gave him the ability to face and overcome his troubles. In contrast to David's response, we read the story of Pharaoh as he continued to hold the Israelites captive in spite of all of the pestilences God brought upon him. As with David, God allowed Pharaoh's son to die because of Pharaoh's sin. David and Pharaoh were both shaken by this discipline. Pharaoh became angry and bitter and his heart became hardened toward God, but David acknowledged his insufficiency. He repented and allowed God to soften his heart. The book of Psalms is a testimony to David's softening process as he became a "man after his [God's] own heart" (1 Sam. 13:14).

Pharaoh determined to outsmart God. Although he repented of his sins long enough to allow the Israelites to leave the land of Egypt, he soon allowed the bitterness to build again, and he pursued the children of Israel. It cost him his life.

We have the same choice today. As we find our lives out of control, we can continue to say, "I can do it myself," or we can say, "God, I can't handle this on my own. I am handing the controls over to You. I'm anxious to see what You can do with this mess."

As we yield the reigns of our life to God, we will become aware of His sufficiency. As Job experienced his property being destroyed, his children being taken from him, and his health deteriorating, he still knew God was faithful as he said, "Though he slay me, yet will I trust in him" (Job 13:15).

The psalmist David states: "I am radiant with joy because of your mercy, for you have listened to my troubles and have seen the crisis in my soul" (Ps. 31:7 TLB).

And God responds: "I want you to trust me in your times of trouble, so I can rescue you, and you can give me glory" (Ps. 50:15 TLB).

One mother wrote: "God and religion were not an important part of my life prior to my son's death. However, during the depths of my depression, I found a new, more personal relationship with God. I pray often and feel He has manifested Himself to me by answering my prayers for help and by comforting me."

Through our pain and suffering we can come to grips with our own insufficiencies and recognize that only God is sufficient to meet our needs. Once we come to that point, we will be able to grow through our grief.

I believe God also desires that we see and understand His sovereignty. Often when people face tragedy, they have to reevaluate their concept of God. When good things happen to us, it is easy to say, "God did this for me." When things happen to us that we perceive as bad, it is hard for us to acknowledge that God could possibly have anything to do with our troubles.

Scripture makes it very clear, though, that some of our difficulties, infirmities, and traumas come so that the Son of God may be glorified:

"And as Jesus passed by, he saw a man which was blind from his birth. And his disciples asked him, saying, Master, who did sin, this man, or his parents, that he was born blind? Jesus answered, Neither hath this man sinned, nor his parents: but that the works of God should be made manifest in him" (John 9:1-3).

God does not originate or orchestrate sin, but I do believe we define some things as bad which are not. For example: For the Christian, death is not bad. "Precious in the sight of the LORD is the death of his saints" (Ps. 116:15). Death is sad for the Christians who are left behind to live in this world without our loved ones, but when a Christian is transported from this world into God's eternal world, there is rejoicing in heaven! "Thou shalt guide me with thy counsel, and afterward receive me to glory" (Ps. 73:24).

The Bible also teaches that God controls (in contrast to "originates") the trouble that comes our way. "But as for you, ye thought evil against me; but God meant it unto good, to bring to pass, as it is this day, to save much people alive" (Gen. 50:20).

James 5:11 states: "You have heard of Job's perseverance and have seen what the Lord finally brought about. The Lord is full of compassion and mercy" (NIV). The Living Bible paraphrase says: "Job is an example of a man who continued to trust the Lord in sorrow; from his experiences we can see how the Lord's plan finally ended in good, for he is full of tenderness and mercy."

It may appear that we are victims of our circumstances, but I don't think that is true. In our case, I believe God knew Nate was going to be in an accident, and He chose not to intervene. We are so quick to judge God when He allows some occurrence in our lives that seems negative to us, but we don't take into account all of the times He has protected us and spared us from tragedy. I have observed that Christians have trouble healing from their grief if they don't accept God's sovereignty and acknowledge that God is involved in the lives of His children; He controls the obvious good and the apparent bad that occur in our lives.

"And the LORD said unto him, Who hath made man's mouth? or who maketh the dumb, or deaf, or the seeing, or the blind? have not I the LORD?" (Ex. 4:11).

"I know, O LORD, that thy judgments are right, and that thou in faithfulness hast afflicted me. Let, I pray thee, thy merciful kindness be for my comfort, according to thy word unto thy servant" (Ps. 119:75-76).

Through suffering we come to know God in all of His greatness, and we come to know ourselves in all of our frailties. We discover we don't have all the answers.

When I was a little girl, my parents and I visited a church in Fort Wayne, Indiana, and I remember a story the pastor told. When he was young, he and his father would stand out on their front porch and view the stars. As they did, the little boy would recite, "Twinkle, twinkle little star. How I wonder what you are." The stars were a beautiful mystery.

Years passed and the young man went on to college. He listened to the professors as they explained the wonders of the universe. Finally, he looked up at the heavens and with an arrogant finger pointed toward the sky and said, "Twinkle, twinkle little star. Now I know what you are!" The stars were now simply a fact of science.

As a middle-aged man, one who had experienced the mysteries and complexities of life and who had begun to recognize God's sovereignty over the universe, he looked up at the stars with great humility and stated, "Twinkle, twinkle little star; how I wonder what you are."

I have traveled a similar path, from not understanding God at all, to thinking I had Him all figured out, to recognizing that although God has let me in on some of His secrets, there are still many things about life and about Him that I will never understand. But after running the gamut of questions and of feelings, I have come to the conclusion that it is important for me to focus on *who God is rather than on what He can, will, or should do.*

When the three Hebrew children were thrown into the fiery furnace, they knew God was capable of rescuing them; however, they did not know whether He would choose to show His power in that way.

> Shadrach, Meshach, and Abednego replied, "O Nebuchadnezzar, we are not worried about what will happen to us. If we are thrown into the flaming furnace, our God is able to deliver us; and he will deliver us out of your hand, Your Majesty. But if he doesn't, please understand, sir, that even then we will never under any circumstance serve your gods or worship the golden statue you have erected.
> (Dan. 3:16-18 TLB)

They focused on who He was, not on what He would do. He is the God who created the universe, numbered my days even before I was formed, and loved me enough to die for me. I serve a great God! If things sometimes don't seem to go according to my plan, it's not that God failed or even necessarily that I failed, but simply that I didn't see His plan. God can see the entire plan for my life and my loved ones' lives all in one quick glance, but I only see a little here and a little there.

" 'For I know the plans that I have for you,' declares the LORD, 'plans for welfare and not for calamity to give you a future and a hope'" (Jer. 29:11 NASB).

Bobbi found my book, *Roses in December*, just a few months after her daughter's death, at a point when she thought she was losing her mind. Today I received a letter from Bobbi and it is so timely, I must share it with you.

"I feel I'm making some real progress at last in dealing with Shannon's death. About a month ago I realized that my asking Why? continually was actually hindering my recovery. I was asking more to protest than for any other reason, and in that way I was making it hard for God to use me and heal me. I have a larger sense of God's peace now."

Suffering comes to all people, but as we surrender to God's power and His sovereignty, He will give us the ability to face our troubles, grow strong through them, and use our experiences for His glory. Oswald Chambers points out: "Suffering is the heritage of the bad, of the penitent, and of the Son of God. Each one ends in the cross. The bad thief is crucified, the penitent thief is crucified, and the Son of God is crucified. By these signs we know the widespread heritage of suffering."[1]

Suffering truly is a universal experience. Some people choose to develop thorns of rebellion, but others display the rose of surrender. Not passive surrender, but the surrender that signifies we have acknowledged there is a Power beyond ourselves who cares for us and controls our world. As we bend our knee to that power and display the rose of willing surrender, a supernatural peace will be ours.

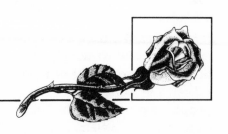

The Rose of Victory

He has put a new song in my mouth —
Praise to our God;
Many will see it and fear,
And will trust in the LORD *(Psalms 40:3* NKJV*).*

When the police came to tell my friend Patsy her daughter Suzie had been in an accident, Patsy sensed it was very serious. Yet as she drove to the hospital, she reasoned, "Everything seems normal. Traffic is moving properly; people are walking down the street; the moon is shining; and the stars are still in the sky. If Suzie were dead, the whole world would stop. Everything would be in chaos—life could not proceed in its normal pattern."

However, when she arrived at the hospital, she discovered Suzie had died, and Patsy's world turned upside down even though the rest of the world did not stop.

I felt the same way after Nate died. I would watch people complacently shopping or enjoying a meal in a restaurant, and I wanted to shout, "How can you do that? Don't you know Nate is dead?"

When you're facing a severe crisis, your world does stop. Nothing matters. Life loses its edge. The big question is, Does the world ever start turning again? You may wonder, *Will little things ever matter? Will I ever get excited about anything? Will I ever enjoy life to its fullest again?*

After Jimmy and Ethan died, we did eventually begin to enjoy life again. I got excited about Christmas for my children, and I did learn to enjoy long-awaited events. But once in a while I still cast a nostalgic look at what might have been.

Whenever I see twins, I wonder what it would have been like to raise Nathan and Ethan together. When I see a large family, I wish I could have raised all five of my children instead of just three. This year Jimmy would have been twenty-nine, and his birthday was difficult for me. As I looked at other young men his age, I felt cheated because I didn't get to watch him grow up.

My heart winces when I hear a mother yell angrily at her children or threaten to "give them away" if they don't behave. I'm tempted to reprove her and say, "You should appreciate your children and thank God you have them."

Our whole family really enjoyed Mellyn's wedding, but even Mellyn remembered the two brothers who were absent. The pillow which held the wedding rings was a satin one used to hold flowers at Ethan's funeral, and the flower girl carried a white wicker basket from Jimmy's funeral. Mellyn explained, "I want all of my brothers to be represented."

We did quite well at Matt's wedding a year and a half

after Nate's death until we posed for a family picture. Then we didn't dare look at each other because we all knew what the others were thinking: *When we had the family picture taken at Mellyn's wedding, Nate was with us. He should be here now.*

As I watched many of Nate's classmates participate in Matt and Debbie's wedding, I wondered if Nate could see. Did he know his big brother married one of his best friends? Oh, how I wished I could talk with him!

As I watched Nate's friend Christian perform with his college glee club, I was thrilled for him, but my eyes filled with tears as I remembered when he and Nate had talked of attending college together.

Afterward, I told his mother how much I enjoyed the concert. Her response helped me a great deal. "I'm sure you enjoyed the program, but I know you must have been thinking what it would have been like to have Nate there because I was thinking about him, too." It feels so good to know others have not forgotten him.

Life is never the same after a loved one has died or you suffer some other major loss. But life can be good again— different, but good. As I look back over the past few years, I can mark turning points in my healing process: The first trip to Hawaii allowed me to step outside of my situation, removed me from some of the pressures, and gave Glen and me time to talk. Moving from full-time to part-time status at the school gave me freedom to spend more time at home and visit with friends when I felt the need to talk. Leaving that position completely finally gave me room to discover some talents in writing and speaking I didn't even know I had.

Another turning point came almost two years after Nate's death. I drove to the cemetery, sat on the grass near Nate's grave, spent some time thinking over the happenings since the accident, and then realized I was getting better. As I walked away, I knew I would not be coming again soon. For me, it was time to move ahead.

Making the decision to speak publicly about my experiences gave me a sense of new beginning and purpose, but it was not easy. Shortly after the funeral I received a card from a representative of MADD. I quickly put the card away and said, "I'll never get involved with any crusades."

Later, Florence Littauer invited me to speak at the HOPE Conference (Helping Other People Emotionally) in Anaheim, California. I worked hard, prepared my notes, and practiced my speech, but the evening prior to the conference I sat in Nate's room and sobbed for hours. I was certain I would break down in the middle of my talk.

Many of my friends attended HOPE, and I asked them to sit in the back of the auditorium so that I wouldn't be affected by their tears. They prayed fervently, and God gave me the strength to present my story without losing control. I was amazed at the response of the people; they said I had really helped them!

Shortly after that I was invited to attend the training for the MADD Speakers' Bureau. I made it clear I was attending simply to gather information; however, to finish the course we were required to present a talk on drunk driving and send a tape of the speech to our trainer. I spoke to the student body at Nate's high school and was thrilled at the students' response. One of the girls in the audience asked me to speak to her youth group, and then someone else invited me to speak at a Kiwanis meeting.

During the next six months I spoke forty-five times to all types of groups from Al-Anon to Kiwanis, to all of the driver's education classes in the San Bernardino City high schools.

Recently I had the privilege of speaking in New Zealand. A woman native to New Zealand told me that while she and her husband were stationed in Germany, their five-year-old son was killed in an electrical accident. There they were, thousands of miles from their families, feeling very alone in their grief.

An acquaintance gave them a German-language version of *Roses in December*. This dear grieving mother was so hungry for help that she read the book, even though she had to translate much of it back into English. She shared that she felt as though my book was her only hope and it helped her in her time of need. One more reminder that our grief wasn't wasted.

Do stories like this make it worth losing my children? *No*, but they help to make their lives and their deaths count. When I think of the other families who have lost a loved one and felt pain similar to mine, nearly 26,000 each year to drunk driving alone since Nate's death, I realize if I can persuade even one person not to drink and drive, if because Nate died, I can save even one family from this pain, or if I can help grieving parents pull their lives back together because Jimmy, Ethan, and Nathan died, I am establishing a living memorial to my boys. That's a rose!

When my friend Diana's ten-year-old son Jimmy died in a shooting accident, Diana was devastated. She had lived in Phoenix only a few months and felt completely alone in her grief. After seeing a program about Compassionate Friends on television, she called the headquarters to find out how to get in touch with a group in her area. She was disappointed to hear there was no chapter in Phoenix, but the national director gave her the name of another bereaved parent who had been trying to start a chapter and suggested Diana help her. Diana thought, "How can I do that? I can't help anybody else; I'm the one who needs help." But Diana did eventually become involved and was a founding member of the Phoenix chapter.

When she moved to Riverside, California, four years after Jimmy's death, Diana started a new chapter of Compassionate Friends. Since that time she has offered a listening ear and given hope to hundreds of bereaved families throughout Southern California. Through her support of other grieving parents, Diana has given purpose and meaning to Jimmy's life and to his death.

Jasmine was born with Down's syndrome, but her parents praised the Lord because tests showed she did not have any heart defects. However, when little Jasmine was five and a half months old, the entire family contracted the flu. Jasmine became very ill and it was soon discovered that she did in fact have two holes in her heart. She died two weeks later of heart failure.

Her mother, Colleen, recalls, "At first I didn't see how I could help anybody else; I was just trying to help myself." Colleen met with a professional counselor regularly for several months and kept good notes on the counseling techniques that helped her the most. After she went back to her position as a childbirth educator, co-workers would call her when a client's child died, saying, "Since you've gone through this, I think you'll know just what to say." Now Colleen frequently counsels with bereaved parents of young infants. She states, "I'd rather have Jasmine back, but there are great rewards in sharing the pain of these parents. It's a memorial to Jasmine's life."

A newly bereaved parent said to me, "It bothers me to think I might become a better person, that I might benefit from my daughter's death. It doesn't seem that anything good should come from a child dying."

I responded, "You have three choices. You could try to stay the same and not have her death affect you; you could give up on life and become a societal dropout; or you can become a stronger, more sensitive, wiser person because your child lived and died."

If you have lost someone you love, you will have to make a choice, too, but don't feel you must rush into any big decisions. Do your grief work. Give yourself time. Seek God's heart, and let Him guide you into the unique purpose He has for you.

It may be months or even years before you realize you are actually enjoying the "ordinary" things of life again. I always enjoyed cooking and entertaining, but after Nate's death, cooking took too much energy and entertaining seemed purposeless. I am slowly learning to enjoy entertaining again, but it's on a different scale. Now I am more interested in what we do than in what we eat.

For example, this past Christmas I invited several of my neighbors to my home for dinner and then I took them all to watch Glen in a Christmas production. My purpose was to help them see the real meaning of Christmas; that Christ offers peace of heart. Therefore, I was comfortable planning a simple meal of store-bought lasagna, salad, and garlic bread. My meal was simple, but the program was very meaningful to each of them.

Before Nate's death, I would have worn myself out cooking lots of special foods and would have been too tired to enjoy the evening's program. My priorities are different now. Before he died, when the children were home, mealtime was always an event. We looked forward to being together and catching up on the news of the day. After Nate's death, Glen and I had difficulty eating at the dining room table when it was only the two of us. Nate's absence was just too obvious. We moved to another room to eat when we were alone. After three years, we moved into a different home, and then we finally were able to establish a pattern of eating in the dining room again.

There will come a day when I can enjoy watching a high school basketball game, and some day I will look forward to Christmas again. Eventually, when someone asks the simple question, "How many children do you have?" I will be able to answer without feeling my stomach churn.

God will lead us to victory, and He does make all things work together for good. I am beginning to see glimpses of that "good."

A few years ago I attended the funeral of another young man who was killed by a drunk driver. I didn't want to go, but I felt I must offer my comfort to his wife and young child. While I was at their home, I met a woman whose children I had known, but I had not met Sandy before. I talked with her and openly shared our loss of Nate and how we were trusting God to get us through this experience.

After the funeral, Sandy came up to me and said, "I need to talk with you."

I said, "Fine, what about?"

Sandy responded, "I'm ready to take a step with God, and I think you can help me!"

That evening, over pie at a local restaurant, I was able to lead my new friend Sandy into a personal relationship with Christ. Through her tears, she commented, "Nate may be gone, but his life lives on." I know her statement is true. The evidences of Nathan's impact on the world are all around me. I see his influence on our friends, on his friends, and on our family. I know Glen and I are stronger people because of what we have faced in the years since Nate's death.

If my boys have the opportunity to look in on me from heaven, I hope they can say, "We may be gone, but our mom is living on. She hasn't given up. She is still serving God, and she is a stronger person who is walking closer to God because she had three sons who lived and died and are now living with God."

Friend, don't give up. As you go through this December of your life, God is willing to walk beside you. He understands when you have hard days; He understands you are grieving because of the terrible loss you've suffered.

Look around you and see the roses: the friend who is standing with you, the memories of your loved one, the Scripture God has given you, the kindnesses others have offered, the work God is doing in your heart. Gather those roses, and let their refreshing aroma fill your life with a confidence that Jesus hears and cares about you. Reach out to the Lord, and put your hand in His so He can lead you to *victory*.

Keep looking for the roses!

Notes

The Rose of Sorrow

1. This quote is generally credited to Sir James Barrie, the author of Peter Pan.

The Rose of Forgiveness

1. S. I. McMillen, M.D., *None of These Diseases* (Westwood, New Jersey: Fleming H. Revell Company, 1963), 73-74.

2. Lewis B. Smedes, "Forgiveness: Healing the Hurts We Don't Deserve," *Family Life Today* ,January 1985, 24-28.

3. Joni Eareckson Tada and Steve Estes, *A Step Further* (Grand Rapids, Michigan: Zondervan Publishing House, 1978), 15-16.

The Rose of Remembrance

1. Joseph Bayly, *The Last Thing We Talk About* (Elgin, Illinois: David C. Cook Publishing Co., 1973), 66.

The Rose of Innocence

1. Janice C. Harris, ACSW-CSW, and Angela Bennett,

"Helping Children Cope with Death in the Family"
(Hurst, Texas: Mothers Against Drunk Drivers, 1984,
pamphlet).

The Rose of Uniqueness

1. Florence Littauer, *Personality Plus* (Old Tappan,
New Jersey: Fleming H. Revell, 1983), 18-20.

2. Ibid.

3. Ibid.

4. Ibid.

5. Lana Bateman, *Personality Patterns* (Dallas, Texas:
Philippian Ministries, 1985), 3-12.

6. Ibid.

7. Ibid.

The Rose of Tenderness

1. Robert L. Veninga, "How to Cope with Heartache," *Ladies Home Journal*, November 1985, 74-82.

The Rose of Confidence

1. Pastor John Emmans, *The Furnace of Affliction* (San
Bernardino, California: CBC Publications, May
1971).

The Rose of Surrender

1. Harry Verploegh, editor, *Oswald Chambers: The Best
from All His Books* (Nashville, Tennessee: Oliver-Nel-
son Books, 1987), 343.

About the Author

Marilyn Heavilin is a wife, mother, grandmother, former high-school counselor, and a frequent speaker on the topics of grief, family life, child-rearing, and the problem of drinking drivers. She is recommended by the speakers' bureaus for Christian Leaders, Authors, and Speakers' Seminars (CLASS) and Mothers Against Drunk Drivers (MADD), and is a frequent speaker for Compassionate Friends, a support group for bereaved parents.

In addition to her speaking commitments, Marilyn helps others improve their speaking skills through her staff position with CLASS. She and her husband, Glen, live in Redlands, California.